Effective

C000258452

The Coaching Process for Climbing Instructors

Mark Reeves MSc, MIA

The contents of this book are copyright to the author and the contributors where noted in the text. The content of this book serves as both a reminder and revision tool for climbing instructors as well as a reference book for Coaching Awards in Climbing. Whilst every attempt has been made to make this as accurate as possible, there may be sections that do not directly apply to the awards or terminology may differ. The author accepts no responsibility for the misuse of the information within and reminds its users of the British Mountaineering Councils participation statement.

"The BMC recognises hat climbing, hill walking and mountaineering are activities with a danger of personal injury or death. Participants in these activities should be aware of and accept these risks and be responsible for their own actions and involvement."

Published by Snowdonia Mountain Guides

ABOUT THE AUTHOR

Mark Reeves is a qualified Mountaineering Instructor and holds an MSc in Applied Sports Science. Based in North Wales for the past 20 years Mark has over 17 years experience in leading groups and coaching climbers both indoors and outdoors on multipitched crags.

He has previously written the self coaching book for climbers called, 'How to Climb Harder' by pesda press and the eBook 'A Mountaineer's Guide to Avalanches' and 'North Wales Climbs' by Rockfax. As well as several coaching and travel articles for the UK climbing press.

Contents

Introduction

Thank you for buying a copy of Effective Coaching: The Coaching Process for Climbing Instructors. The book was compiled by Mark Reeves, an experienced mountaineering instructor and climbing coach, who in 2006 reached a ceiling of rock climbing qualifications in the UK and whilst he knew a little about the coaching process he also felt there was a lot more to learn.

Enrolling on an MSc in Applied Sports Science, Mark studied effective coaching, sports psychology and performance physiology. He also completed 6 months supervised experience coaching mental skills to an elite group of young climbers in North Wales.

This book is a combination of what Mark has learnt, both in studying effective coaching and the real world practice of teaching thousands of people to rock climb over a 17 year period. It is a perfect accompaniment to his first book 'How To Climb Harder' published by Pesda Press.

Mark was also a key author of a report into Coaching in Mountaineering for a National Source Group that was established by the British Mountaineering Council and UK Mountain Training Boards. The result of that report was the decision to develop coaching awards in rock climbing. This book is aimed at helping coaches both old and new to develop better coaching practices, as well as fulfilling a current gap in literature that links effective coaching practices to climbing.

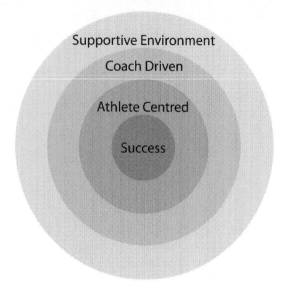

Supportive Environment

Coach Driven

Athlete Centred

Success

1 - The Coaching Process

Coaching for many is seen as a dark art, however our understanding comes from years of both antidotal observations and empirical research into teaching people a skill. Its first application was in the military, when after the First World War it was seen as vital to be able to quickly train troops in the art of warfare. However the concept of teaching and learning has long been part of the human race as parents 'educate' their children to learn about threats in their environment so they can avoid them and survive.

This book however concentrates on the science of what we know about how a person can learn and on the basis of this examines how we can best teach people. To this end the book starts with the psychological processes of how we learn and the stages of learning we go through, before moving onto how anxiety can effect the learning process. This is an important aspect to consider given that coaching climbing can involve putting our students into potentially high risk and high anxiety situations.

By examining the various models of how anxiety effects performance, we make some suggestions as to how anxiety disrupts or limits the learning process. Finally making some recommendations as how a coach can minimise these adverse effects.

We then move on to reverse the theory of how people learn by applying it to how we can teach. This teaching section covers many aspects of coaching and includes several examples of different teaching models and where they can be applied. We then examine the core building blocks of those models from how to introduce a skill, how we can set up what is termed 'effective practice' and through to how to observe and analyze someones performance before giving appropriate feedback. This is the core part of the coaching process when it comes to skill acquisition.

In the next chapter we examine other aspects of advanced coaching in terms of communicating effectively with our students. Looking at the styles of leadership in coaching and how a coach can adapt to develop a team or small group of climbers. We also explore how we can foster good relationships with our students before finally looking at the legal and moral aspects of coaching climbing.

The final chapter looks at reflective practice and describes several classic models for carrying out this important part of coaching. Where the coach explores their own coaching practice and chooses to question what they are doing, why they are doing it and how they are achieving their aims or not.

Hopefully by the end of this book, you will realise that whether you are a instructor, guide or top-rope supervisor, you already coach you just didn't know it. You will able to explain why certain approaches to teaching basic skills work and more importantly you'll be better equipped to experiment with your coaching to improve your practice.

There are more skills to the coaching process than are covered in this book, however this book concentrated on the 'processes' of coaching skills and developing good coaching practices. The skills in this book, whilst focused on climbing are generic skills and can be applied to any skill that you want to teach or learn.

Further books in the series

There are further books to this series, one is only available in printed form from Pesda Press and was written by the author and is called 'How to climb harder', this book gives a good overview to teaching movement, safety techniques, tactical decisions, mental skills and the physiology of training. Which if used in conjunction with this eBook will help turn you into a well rounded coach.

In the future we hope to bring together further publications in the following fields:

- Effective Coaching: Mental Skill for Climbing Coaches

- Effective Coaching: Training Techniques for Climbing Coaches

- A Mountaineers Guide to Avalanches - available in Kindle and iPad formats

In the meantime the author has developed a coaching library for both instructors, coaches and climbers to highlight the best of the web in terms of coaching articles and blog posts. It works like a wiki engine in that you can add to the database of sources and link them to various categories. The library is found at iCoachClimbing.com. There is also a coaching wiki, that too is designed as a digital stop gap for information on how to coach various aspects of climbing.

If you'd like to attend one of the authors CPD courses you can do by visiting Snowdonia Mountain Guides Continuing Professional Development pages.

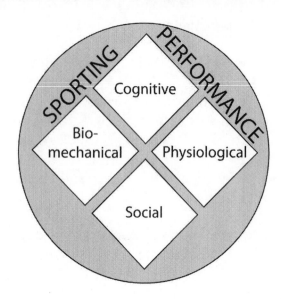

2 - What Is Coaching?

This might seem like a daft question, however the definition of a coach is something that is of growing importance as more people elect to call themselves 'climbing coaches', but what does it mean? Or more importantly, what should it mean?

Definitions of a Coach

1. Someone in charge of training an athlete or a team.
2. A person who gives private instruction.
3. A Sports Coach provides information on the many topics related to developing physical and mental conditions to help fitness enthusiasts, athletes and other coaches achieve their goals and to assist students studying sport related qualifications.
4. The guided improvement of participants in a single or multiple sports and relevant to the identifiable stages of participants biological and physical development.

What is a Coach?

The term coaching stems from the english word of a coach as a form of transport, its origins as a word to mean a tutor or teacher came from Oxford. Where is was a slang term for a university tutor who "carried" his student through the exams. It has come to mean a lot more today and there are numerous definitions based on the many forms of coaching that now occur (life, business, sport, etc...).

However we shall use a definition of a sports coach from a SportsScotland publication on a coaching strategy for Edinburgh 2004.

'A sports coach means a deliverer of all forms of physical activity, which through organised participation, aims at expressing and/or improving motor literacy, physical fitness and mental well-being, forming social relationships or obtaining results in competitions at all levels'.

A further refinement of this would be that coaching focuses on four generic areas that can be worked on to enhance performance:

- Cognitive Skills (reading a route, tactics, staying calm under pressure, mental skills, etc...)

- Biomechanical Skills (Clipping a quickdraw, efficient movement, belaying, etc...)

- Physiological Skills (Stamina, strength, flexibility, etc...)

- Social Skills (Team work, supporting others, trust, etc...)

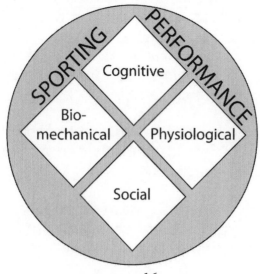

An Alternative to these is often refered to in coaching as TTPP, or:

- Technical

- Tactical

- Physical

- Psychological

Which ever you prefer to use is fine, as it comes down to simple terminology. Although the author prefers the first as it includes the social skill dimension.

Whilst most coaches have an area of speciality within these four areas, they still use a broad spectrum of coaching interventions to help students improve their performance. However the skill of the coach comes in choosing which of these areas will best suit the needs of an individual and it is this focus on an individual that separates coaching from teaching. As teaching is seen as more of a mass educational tool, rather than a person specific application.

Instructor, Guide or Coach?

In climbing, throughout the world there are various qualifications available that qualify people to teach rock climbing in a variety of different environments. From guiding up a alpine peak, to instructing people on multipitch rock climbs, to supervising total beginners climbing indoors and through to coaching national squads.

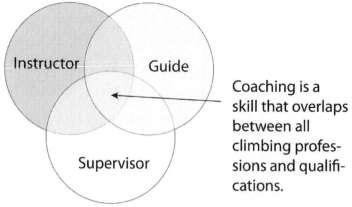

Coaching is a skill that overlaps between all climbing professions and qualifications.

Each of these professional climbing qualifications, be it a guide, instructor, teacher or supervisor, all have an interest in coaching climbing. However many people have debated who is the best at coaching. To be honest there are no doubt good and bad examples of 'coaching behaviours' within all of these examples. So rather than get hung up on which of these is more suited to coaching, instead view them as inter-linked, where the overlap is the coaching element of what they all do.

Whatever your qualification, if you teach climbing you undoubtably coach. Throughout this book you will no doubt come across ideas and techniques that you use. You may have picked them up from observing others, developed them through unconscious or conscious trial and error or even been taught them as part of a course.

What is important to the coaching process is that you accept that there will be areas you understand and excel at, whilst there are other areas that you might not even be aware of and therefore need developing. The last chapter on reflective practice covers this in detail, however as you move through this book I hope you find some new skills and techniques to become the best coach you can be.

Skill Acquisition

There is a fifth generic skill to coaching, one that is not covered in that model we have shown and that is the ability to help climbers acquire skill. This book covers the process of coaching from this skill acquisition point of view, as well as some of the social implications a coach needs to understand to be more effective. These teaching skills are applicable to all areas of performance. So whether you are teaching mental skills, movement skills, tactics, teamwork or focused on the physical side of training. These lessons can be applied to move someone from a novice to an expert.

This book shows the current understanding of coaching behaviours and practice. Which when applied to teaching skills will help you to improve the performance of your students. As such this book focuses on the process of teaching, learning and developing individuals and teams.

Primarily we use an 'athlete centred' approach to coaching. Where success lies with coaching being athlete centred, coach driven and are framed within supportive environment that includes senior coaches, parents, club and other interested parties. This is possibly one of the most fundamental things we need to remember as a coach. We are there for our clients benefits not our own. That is not to say that coaching is not rewarding, just that success can be measured in many ways, be it getting a frightened novice to the top of a climb or helping a seasoned climber to red-point the hardest route of their life. The coach often has to live vicariously through the achievements of their students.

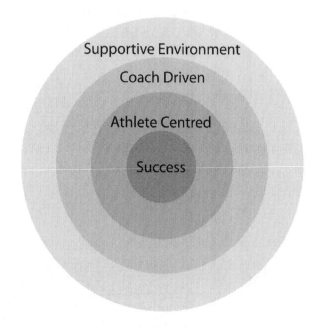

Coaching Qualifications

At the time of writing there are a couple of nationally recognised coaching qualifications in climbing within the UK. These are the foundation and development coach.

Whilst these are predominantly aimed at coaching indoors, if used in conjunction with the existing out-door awards like the Single Pitch Award or Moun-tain Instructor Awards will give the holder a greater knowledge base to coach in the terrain their existing qualification allows them to..

This book covers the generic coaching process that can be applied to any of these awards as well as covering other accreditation schemes like the Wilderness Education Association Instructor/Guide scheme in the United States.

Other performance coaching schemes have been developed by elite climbers like Neil Gresham's Master Class Academy. Whilst other coaches like the author chose to follow a more pracademic route by studying sports science at either undergraduate or post graduate degree level and gain nationally recognised awards alongside.

All of these pathways mean that different coaches will have specialised in different areas of coaching. Hopefully when the new coaching awards come out it will allow more climbing instructors and coaches to meet a nationally recognised standard of coaching. This book covers some of the syllabus of these new awards that are not currently found in the Mountain Training textbooks.

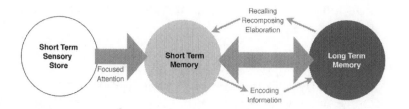

3 - Understanding Learning

In understanding the psychological processes of how people learn, coaches are better able to understand how to teach people a skill. It is this understanding of learning that forms the basis of how individuals can acquire new skills and develop existing ones.

Introduction to learning

As a coach it is our responsibility to teach or encourage certain skills, techniques and behaviours from our clients. It therefore figures that in order to be most effective at teaching skills we need to understand the process of learning so we can reverse engineer our coaching to meet the needs of any learner.

In this chapter we look at various learning models, all have aspects to them that are important to gaining a better understanding of how people learn. However some of them are overly simple and serve only as an introduction to the subject.

The real understanding of how people learn comes when we introduce the psychological processes humans employ when they are engaged in learning. In understanding this underlying process of learning we come to see the fundamental principles of memory and therefore how as a coach we can achieve the best teaching results.

Basic Learning Models

These basic learning models are included to help frame your understanding of learning through ways you may have been presented or taught them in the past. Similarly if you are faced with trying to teach people the basic concepts of how people learn starting with an easier model can greatly simplify the concept.

The Learning Curve

The concept of the learning curve was developed in 1984 by Whitmore and it associated the level of understanding a learner has to execute holistically the act of climbing as a whole. It supposes that we travel through 4 stages of learning.

Unconsciously Incompetent - A student is unaware they are not competent in a a skill.

Consciously Incompetent - A student becomes conscious they are not competent, at this point learning can start.

Consciously Competent - A student has become competent in a skill but needs to think and concentrate on what they are doing in order to maintain their performance.

Unconsciously Competent - A student can demonstrate they are competent at a skill and can carry it out without thinking about it.

When we trace someone's perceived ability, that is how well someone thinks they are performing, we see that when someone starts in a new skill they are **Unconscious** of the fact they are **Incompetent**, often thinking they are better than they are. However as soon as someone becomes **Conscious** of there **Incompetence** they perceive a drop in their performance. At this point a student can start to learn as a level of self awareness has been reached. After practicing a skill over time that learner can become **competent** at that skill if they remain **conscious** of what they are doing. In that they have to think through every part of the skill. Finally given enough time and practice of a skill a student can become **unconsciously competent**. In that they can perform competently without having to think consciously about it.

This if you like is a very simplified version of the stages of learning, and associated level of performance. As we will see later this is a simplified model but one that can reflect situations where a students performance suddenly drops after initially trying a new skill or technique.

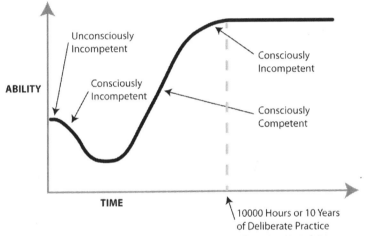

Skill Versus Technique

Before we continue it is important that we define and separate a skill from a technique. A technique is any task performed in isolation. A skill is the ability to perform that technique in a more contextual performance setting. So whilst it might be possible for someone to perform an isolated technique close to ground in a controlled setting what we want to be able to do is take that technique and help people apply it skillfully in a real climbing setting. In coaching it is important to make sure a technique can be performed first before adding it into a more skillful climbing performance setting.

Learning Cycle's

There are many examples of learning cycles, often developed by many different people, for many different ends. As such some have more relevance to us than others. There are certainly times where each of these can be used to give a simplified model of learning or be applied when teaching in certain ways, especially when using what is described as experiential learning.

Experiential Learning

This is about learning from the direct experience of the student. This can be a totally organic form of learning through open trial and error by the student; or alternatively through carefully managed or staged lessons, as a form of what is called guided discovery.

3 Stage Cycle

The three stage model of learning is the most simple and is best explained by giving an example of how it can be applied. A student may approach a boulder problem and look at it, this is the 'planning' phase of the cycle. Next the student attempts to climb the problem, this is the 'doing' phase. Whether they are successful or not they may take time to reflect on what went right or what went wrong, the reviewing phase. This review can then be fed back into the planning phase and the cycle of learning continues.

However this cycle, can also be viewed as a more complex system where each Plan-Do-Review cycle leads to greater learning and understanding. If visualised as a spiral the bigger the surface area/longer the spiral the greater the learning that has occurred.

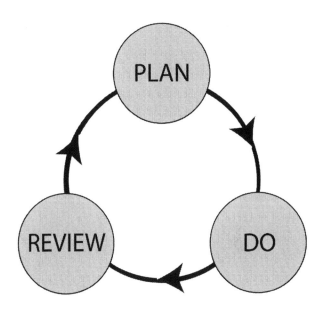

At times the student might make a step backwards and re-examine or re-evaluate their learning. This was dubbed the learning spiral by the author in How to Climb Harder.

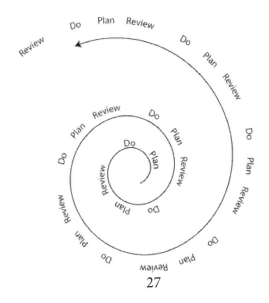

Accelerated Learning Cycle

The accelerated learning cycle is really just another version of the three stage model, however it takes into account more 'real world' learning as it pulls in other aspects of what the coach can do to help the learner.

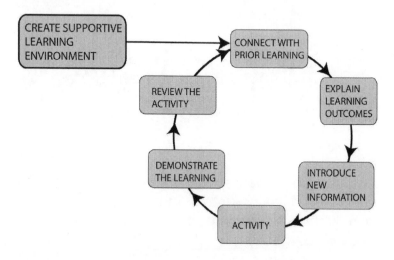

The first phase of this cycle is the creation of a supportive and positive learning environment, which whilst in the most part is down to the us the coach. Often it is also about developing a team that knows how to nurture each other. In climbing, as we shall see later this can also be seen as choosing a learning environment that is appropriate for both the individual and the skill you are teaching and where possible managing that environment to minimise anxiety.

Having selected or created a suitable learning environment, we then need to get our students to connect to prior learning. Even if someone is an absolute beginner there are always examples where we can give an analogy to the activity or help a student remember previous lessons. This is part of the introduction or build up to the lesson.

An example might be teaching a simple rock over and explain to the group that they perform a rockover every time they stand up from a seat without using their arms or walking up a flight of stairs without using the bannister.

Another important part of this connecting to prior learning, is to put the skill into its context. So if we use the example of a rock-over again, then we can explain to people that the rock-over is one of the fundamental skills of climbing movement and its about transferring weight from one point of balance to the next. Often tagged onto the end of this is the explanation of what we expect people to achieve in the session or individual lesson.

We can then show them what they need to do and allow the group time to process that. In essence we have split the planning phase down into 3 parts, as well as added the creation of a supportive learning environment.

The next phase is doing phase and again we have spilt this into two. The first is simply the activity, where a climber can be left to go through many mini cycles of Plan-Do-Review, before you the coach asks them to demonstrate what they have learnt.

Finally, we get the student to recall and review what they have done, to help them retain those lessons. This method works particularly well with more experiential learning or guided discovery. Where the student is encouraged to learn through doing and self experimentation.

Again this is a simplified model, but one that helps adds a variety of views and opinions in teaching, coaching and instruction.

Learning Styles

Kolb was a proponent of experiential learning and he develop the following model that takes into account how we think about things and how we do things. (see diagram below)

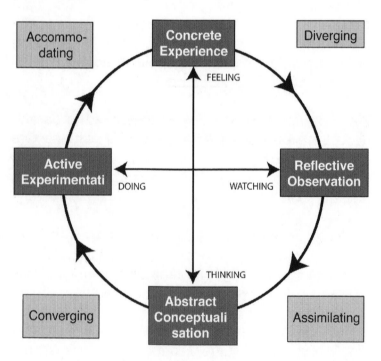

How we think has two ends of the thinking spectrum, 'Concrete Experience', in this model it is described as what we feel. At the other end of this spectrum is 'Abstract Conceptualisation' and is the thinking of new ideas.

On the doing spectrum there is 'Active Experimentation' the actual doing of an activity or hands on problem solving. Whilst at the other end is the 'Reflective Observation' or the watching others or reflecting on your own experience.

As well as these two spectrums, Kolb suggests that there are set ways to travel round his learning styles. The diverging learner combines the feeling and watching aspects of either spectrum. The assimilator combines watching and thinking. The Converging learner takes the thinking and doing aspect. Finally the accomodator combines the feeling and doing.

Despite this rather complicated model there are some more simplistic things we can take out of it, that are basic parts of learning, in that learning requires thinking, watching, doing and feeling. As we will see in the next part on more psychological ideas of learning.

VACK Learning

A simpler way to view Kolb's learning styles is that as individuals people can have preferences as to how they take on information and process it. So some people learn through either seeing, hearing/reading, doing and feeling. Lastly Kolb's idea that we can analytically think through processes and problems, means that there is also a cognitive side to learning.

This means there are Visual, Audio, Cognitive and Kinesthetic aspects to learning. However there is very little scientific support for the notion that people have a preferred delivery method. It is more likely that everybody switches between all four when learning, often dependent on what is being learnt. To this end we will see in the teaching models that we cover, all these learning pathways are included.

Psychology of Learning

The psychological side of learning is a little different to these more simple models that are more aimed at developing experiential learning. Often this experienced based learning approach is used in 'Outdoor Education', where the outdoors is used as a vehicle for teaching more key life skills like personal and social development. As it allows children to learn through direct experience.

This psychological approach looks at the processes that occur in the brain and how the student interacts with these in order to learn.

Before we explain these processes lets first use an example of learning to explore the mechanism. For this we shall use a simple activity using a ball and a bin. To start with we shall say that we are going to throw the ball into the bin underarm from a distance of around 5 metres.

If you had the ball in your hands your attention is now drawn towards both the feeling of the ball in your hand, it's size, shape and weight. Possibly followed by the distance to the bin, the size and shape of the target. All this helps you best guess the required trajectory.

You throw the ball and you miss, but in your mind you are already recalculating the necessary trajectory alterations to succeed. You alter your next throw and you bounce it off the rim this time. You go through process of refinement again and after a few more goes you are now becoming a lot more accurate, regularly getting the ball in the bucket.

Have you learnt a skill of throwing the ball in the bucket? Probably not, instead you have learnt a technique to get the ball in the bucket if you throw underarm from 5 metres.

I now get you to repeat the same task but this time I get you to throw the ball over arm. Whilst you have some recent experience in terms of how much force is needed and you might be able to conceptualise a better trajectory, you still need trial and error to get the ball in the bucket.

In both cases you have programmed a part of your brain to accomplish this very closed task, however in each case you have probably only stored the engram or motor control program in your short term memory.

Next I ask you to get the ball in your hand and at random I ask you to throw the ball either underarm or overarm, but you don't know whether it will be one or the other until you are about to throw the ball.

In this third case you have to send the engram or movement program from your short term memory to long-term memory and after you know what way you are going to throw, fetch the appropriate movement from you long-term memory to short-term memory. It is this process of encoding from short-term to long-term memory and then rebuilding it from long-term to short-term, where learning occurs as we create better memory traces in our brain.

However there is another aspect of this system that is called the short-term sensory store. This if you like is how we access the world through our five senses (Sight, Touch, Hearing, Smell & Taste). I eluded to it at the beginning of the example, when I suggested you focus you attention on the ball and the bin.

What we are about to look at is how these various systems work and how we as coaches can start to use them to the best advantages of learning.

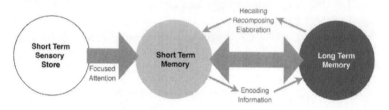

The Learning Brain

The learning brain is still something of a simplified model of how we learn. However if you understand these fundamental principles of learning, then it is possible to work up from these and find the logic within the later chapters on both learning, anxiety and teaching models.

Perhaps a modern and easy analogy of the learning

brain, is that it is like a computer. With inputs from a mouse, keyboard, microphone, WIFI or webcam. These all go to a processors like graphics card, USB card, WIFI card or sound cards, in the brain these specific processors are parts of the short-term sensory store.

That information is filtered and passed on to be processed by a Central Processing Unit and RAM, this is the main computer processor. For each piece of information you send there is a single application that the computer is running. As we know most computers can only run a few programs before they become very slow or crash. This part of the brain is called short-term memory and has similar limitations in term of the amount of processing power it has.

These applications can then send information to a hard disk, a CD or other storage device to be retrieved when needed and our short term memory can do the same to by sending information to be encoded in our long-term memory. Applications can also output information text graphic or sound. Just like our short-term can make us speak, move or think.

Short-Term Sensory Store

The short-term sensory store is a simplification of many systems we have in our brain, one deals in terms of what is dubbed the visuo-spacial sketchpad or iconic memory (Visual information). Another similar system works for hearing and is part of our echoic memory (Auditory information). There is a further system that deals with feelings of touch or our haptic memory (Kinesthetic information) and finally there are other memory sensory systems for smell and taste. Arguably there is also a system for our feelings or emotional memory. For the purpose of skill acquisition, we will focus on the Visual, Auditory and Kinesthetic information.

Lets explore these systems, wherever you are right now, stop reading at the end of this paragraph, and take a moment to see just what is going on around you. As until the point that you turn your focus away from this text, you will be blanking out any unnecessary information that your senses are constantly collecting. So take a minute or two to switch your focus from an internal point to an external one, from sights to sounds to feelings.

As you switched your focus what you noticed will no doubt have altered and changed but essentially all that information is being processed all the time, our brain just decides to ignore most of it. What is important to learners though is that they learn to or you help them to focus on the bits of information they need to be aware of to learn a skill. This becomes important when we move onto the short term memory.

The Short-Term Sensory Store has what some theorised to be an almost unlimited amount of information it can store for only microseconds, to a limit of around 20 to 30 pieces of information that it can store for just under two seconds. Either way there is a limit in this cognitive part of learning and that limit is time rather than quantity of information. In order to use that information we need to choose to focus our attention on the right bits of information at the right time.

Short-Term Memory

Short-term memory is the working memory we use to process information both coming into the brain from what we choose to focus on from our short-term sensory store and what is coming out from our long-term memory.

Various scientific studies have shown that this particular part of the brain can store and hold information for up to several seconds. If we don't run through that information over and over, then after those few seconds without thinking about it the information soon fades.

Research has also found there is a limit to the amount of information we can store in short term memory and that is often described as the magical number 7+/-2. One of the reasons this varies, we will look at in the next chapter. However for now just accept that at times we can hold more or less information based on how much short term memory we have available at any given time.

In learning and coaching this is perhaps the biggest barrier we have to learn to adapt to. As giving people more than those 7+/-2 pieces of information they become overloaded and unable to focus on everything at once. As such when we are teaching we have to be wary not to give students too much information.

However, there is a way that short term memory works that we as coaches can use to help us overcome this problem of information overload to a certain extent. This is best illustrated with this example below, look at the list of letters below for 5 seconds and then look away. After that try to write down all the letters, or simply recall them.

TWAAIDSAICFBILRIGDNAYOB

The chances are that you didn't succeed in this task, although you may have started to chunk some of the information, especially if you are over 30 and remember that twa was an airline, similarly aids is a disease, aic, is cia backwards, followed by fbi and the last part is boy and girl in reverse. Now we have structured that information differently, you can chunk bits together and recall more information, but in essence we are still only limited to those 7+/-2 pieces of information, although in this case the information is in larger chunks.

An example of how we can utilise this 'chunking' in climbing is teaching belaying. At first the process of belaying takes several distinct and complicated steps. However it can be quick chunked into taking in the rope, locking the rope off, and swapping your hands back to the start. Then maybe chunked further to simply take in, lock off, hand swap. Finally a climber will just belay, as it essentially becomes one simple chunk. By structuring the information differently we are able to process more of it..

Long-Term Memory

Our long term-memory is where we send all the encoded information from our short-term memory. If you like it is a massive filing cabinet that stores everything from how to ride a bike through to what you had to eat last saturday.

Whilst the Short-term sensory store has a problem with the fleeting nature of the information it can store and short-term memory is limited to those 7+/-2 chunks of information. Long-term memory also has an achilles heel, in that with so much information, re-trieving the right piece at the right time can become a problem.

However, if you know how that information is stored and how we can strengthen our memory of new skills and new ideas. Then as a coach you can utilise this knowledge to help strengthen your students learning.

Firstly long-term memory stores information in two main ways, one is referred to as explicit memory and the other illicit memory. Explicit memory are the thoughts we can access consciously, whereas illicit memory is only accessible sub-consciously.

Explicit memory, is spilt into two sub types of memo-ry one is episodic and the other is semantic. Episodic memory is best seen as a kind of autobiography of life's events. If you like remembering mini episodes of the soap opera that is your life. Semantic memory is the storing of factual information, often ordered in a structured way through linking a piece of information with a back story or situation.

The Illicit memory is also referred to as procedural memory and it stores information of how we move or interact with objects in our world. If we are trying to teach movement it is this memory into which we are trying to place good movement. It is important to remember that if someone already climbs, then we as coaches have to try and possibly undo bad movement memory.

A final form of memory is emotional memory and this can be linked to all of these different forms of memories. Whilst we might be able to access at will, memories that illicit an emotional response. Those emotional responses are beyond our control, although arguably we can re-train how we respond emotionally to a memory or situation.

As a coach it is important to remember how we store information in our brain. So if we are trying to get someone to remember some form of factual information. Then associating that fact with a story can help reinforce the information. Similarly, at the end of the day or session getting a group or individuals to recount the day as it happened and note down the key learning points will make them recall that information from the episodic memory as it was presented to them and again strengthen those memories by adding a semantic structure.

When it comes down to that procedural memory, it becomes more tricky as it takes between 50-150 repetitions of a movement before it starts to become an illicit or subconscious movement. Until that point we still have to have some form of conscious thinking involved, however with each try more and more of the skill becomes sub-conscious. This is the essence of our next topic where we explore the stages of learning.

Stages of Learning

If we look back at the first learning model we covered then you can see that in that model there were four stages of learning; Unconscious incompetence, Conscious incompetence, Conscious competent and Unconsciously competent.

Again there are many different thoughts about how many stages of learning we go through in our journey from never having done something to being an expert.

We are going to cover a broad spectrum and comment on how they can be applied to coaching climbing and mountaineering. The first is an american system that was developed by Bloom and features a taxonomy of learning verbs each one reflects a level of learning and understanding. This is a rather complex system and instead I will then offer a 3 stage model that was put forward by Fitts and Posner. This focus's solely on motor skill development and fits better with the skill acquisition required for climbing. After that I cover a few more examples of the stages of learning to add completeness.

Bloom's Taxonomy of Learning Verb's

This theory posits the notion that we can gauge the extent of someone's learning and the level they are at through what are described as measurable verbs. This system has limited application to climbing as it was primarily develop for more 'classroom' based learning, however it can be used to assess someones understanding of what they know through questioning. It may be of use for coaches training or assessing other coaches to help understand how well a trainee coach has developed an understanding of the coaching process or more conceptual safety issues.

They suggested there are 6 stages of learning that highlight the level to which a learner can think through a problem. In particular we are interested in getting learners to the last three stages of learning, as they represent a point where the learner can 'critically' think about a problem.

1. Knowledge

2. Comprehension

3. Application

4. Analysis

5. Synthesis

6. Evaluation

Knowledge

The learner is able to recall the specifics of a skill or lesson. You can assess this by asking questions that use the verbs: define, describe, enumerate, identify, label, list, repeat, recall, relate, record or underline.

You can help people in this stage start by highlighting key vocabulary and the basic building blocks of the skill. Similarly mnemonic devices to help them learn the basics.

Comprehension

The learner has started to gain a basic understanding of the skill and can put the idea into their own words. You can assess whether someone has reach this level of learning by asking questions with the following verbs: discuss, explain, restate, trace, express, translate, Identify, describe, tell, locate, report, review or recognise

To help a learner in this stage of learning you can get them to explain a skill or concept to a classmate. Get them to associate skill with prior knowledge or have them summarize key concepts from coaching sessions.

Application

When a learner can apply a general principle to a new and concrete situation, they have started to understand the lessons to reasonable level. Although we are not half way through the stages in this model, this is still a good level of understand for a learner to have developed. Again you can assess whether someone has reached this stage by asking questions with the following verbs: illustrate, classify, compute, predict, relate, solve, utilize, use, employ, interpret, dramatize, sketch, practice, illustrate, operate, demonstrate, apply or schedule.

You can help a learner in this stage of learning by getting them to generate original places to apply a skill in or getting them to solve and analyze new problems that can be overcome with the skills they have. Alternatively get them to predict ways that a new skills will help them in their climbing.

Analysis

The learner can break the information or skill into its component parts in order to explore it and develop different conclusions. In the eyes of this theory the learner has reached a stage where they can critically think through an idea and in essence reach their own conclusions.

Again we can assess whether someone has reached this stage of learning by asking questions with the following verbs: contrast, generalize, illustrate, diagram, differentiate, outline, compare, distinguish, differentiate, diagram, analyze, categorize, appraise, experiment, test, contrast, inspect, debate, inventory, question, examine, criticise, solve or calculate

We can help students develop this stage of learning by getting them to generate comparison and contrast lists and use these to predict new ways to us existing skills. Similarly getting them to identify themes or trends from text, skills or case studies and subsequently organize material in more than one way.

Synthesis

At this stage of learning the student can creatively or divergently apply prior knowledge and skills to produce a new or original whole. You can assess whether a learner has reached this stage by using verbs like: categorise, contrast, design, formulate, generate, design a model, (re)construct, plan, compose, propose, arrange, assemble, collect, create, organise, set up, manage or prepare.

You can help a learner reach and develop in this stage by asking them to predict ways in which the skills they know can be applied in other areas and how they can modify a skill to this new application. Similarly you can get them to locate evidence to support this new idea.

Evaluation

At this top level of understanding a student can judge the value of material and the skills they have based on informed personal values/opinions resulting in an end product without a distinct right or wrong answer. They will be able to apply all their skills to new situations in an appropriate and well thought out manner. You can assess whether a learner has reached this level of learning by asking questions with the following verbs: appraise, conclude, justify, criticize, defend, support, estimate, score, select, rate, choose, measure or revise

You can help a learner in this stage by getting them to list supporting evidence of how and why to apply a skill in a certain setting, as well as list evidence to the contrary. They could generate concept maps and debate the strengths and find weaknesses in other's arguments.

Fitt's and Posner - 3 Stage Model

In 1967 Fitt's and Posner proposed a three stage process for learning motor skills, as such it is much more applicable to how we view learners in motor development and physical activities like rock climbing. The three stages are the conscious phase, the associative phase and the autonomous phase. Each phase has different aspects that we can take into account to help a learner move through the stages of learning.

An important thing to remember is that climbing requires a wide and diverse set of skills to perform and indoor climbing requires different skills to sports climbing. With traditional climbing requiring some different skills to both. As such someone might be in the autonomous stages of skill in one part of their climbing and in the cognitive stages in another. As such part of the coaches role is to try and level that playing field out and get as many skills as possible into the autonomous stage.

Cognitive Stage of Learning

In this phase the learner is developing the basic movement patterns required to achieve a skill. As such it requires a high degree of cognitive activity and attentional demands, all aimed at movement production. In essence we are trying to get students into the ball park of the movement we are looking for. However those high demands on the brain mean that we really need to be aware of those 7+/-2 pieces of information when teaching people in this stage of learning. Similarly blocked practice (see Teach Models chapter) is a good way to move learners most quickly through this stage of learning.

Typically learners who are in this stage of learning will exhibit movements that lack synchronization and may appear choppy or deliberate. As such it will lack what might be described as fluid or flowing movement. Any errors will probably be numerous and typically gross in nature. However the learner will lack the capability to determine causes of an errors or how to correct them.

As such in this stage of learning using questions as a coaching tool are inappropriate. Instead much more coaching comes from us the coach to the learner. If possible trying to call on prior learning or experiences the learner might have to help get them into the general movements patterns we are trying to get them to attain.

Associative Stage of Learning

The associative stage of learning is generally seen as a place where the refinement of movement patterns occurs. The movements tend to be much more consistent and the learner has started to develop engrams or movement memory. So they are now starting to chunk much more information about a movement together, as such the attentional demands of the skill become reduced.

As well as being fewer in number, errors will also be less gross and more refined. Those errors that do occur may well be detected by the student who may be able to detect the cause. As such the student might start developing an appropriate way to correct those errors.

In this stage of learning the use of more complex practice strategies like random, varied, augment or even bi-lateral practice, (see Teaching Models chapter) will help the learner to apply the developing skill to a variety of appropriate environments.

Again as the learner has started to understand the skill more, a limited amount of questioning can be used within the coaching. Similarly a learner will now be able to associate a skill with a general place, time and environment in which it is appropriate to use that skill.

Autonomous Stage of Learning

In this stage of learning a skill is performed almost automatically, as such the student will be on autopilot and the cognitive load will be minimal. The performance will be at the highest level for a specific skill. Not all learners will reach this stage, as it takes very deliberate practice and time to reach this stage of learning.

Because the movement has become automatic and generally consistent the learner can instead turn more attention to strategic decisions. So having moved someone into a high stage of learning for individual skills, we can now start to develop tactical decision making.

The learner will be confident in their ability to perform at this level and the errors will be few and much harder to detect. However the learner will developed a way of detecting those errors and correcting them when they do occur.

In this stage of learning much more complex practice strategies should be used. Like getting the learner to try applying their skills in new and unfamiliar places. Coaching may well take on a much more question-ing form to facilitate the learner to ask themselves the right questions of performance. Similarly video coaching may become more useful, as the mistakes will be much harder to detect by eye alone.

The Five Stage Observational Model of Skill Acquisition

This model was proposed by Lo el Collins an adven-ture sports coach and lecturer at the University of Central Lancaster for observing stages of learning. The model suggests that the 3 stage model is over simplified and there are more stages to learning. In addition to this within each of those stages there are cognitive, biomechanical and physiological compo-nents that can be observed. Those five stages of learning are:

- Awareness

- Practice

- Technical

- Skilled

- Skillful

Awareness

The learner understands what you suggest and can see's its relevance but has yet to apply it. As such the the student has bought into the ideas you are suggesting and their performance is their interpretation of the rules and routines you the coach gave them. The performance will tend to be inconsistent and the learner is only aware of the skill you are teaching them.

Cognitive: A basic understanding of the skill is demonstrated by the students identifying the skill in other's performance. They will be generally unaware of their surroundings and other influences like anxiety on their performance.

Bio-mechanical: Actions will be exaggerated and mistakes common and gross in nature.

Physiological: The performance will be inefficient and fatigue will set in quickly during the activity, resulting in tiredness and muscle soreness.

Practice

The learner is starting to explore what you suggest and see if it works. As a result they will have started to put together components of the skill. With the support of the coach or with both careful planning and time to prepare the student can use elements of the skill or theory. The learner is still using explicit rules set out by the coach as the template and slowly getting a feel for the activity. Performances will be inconsistent and inaccurate, mistakes should still be easy to identify.

Cognitive: The student can describe what they are doing and understand the major influences from the immediate environment on their performance.

Bio-mechanical: The fine detail of the movement will be poorly timed or ordered. The bigger picture of the activity is starting to become appropriate. The skill may look rushed, too slow or erratic.

Physiological: The student may put too much or too little effort into the activity, resulting in a tiring performance. This can effect the length of a session.

Technical

If the learner plans ahead and everything goes to plan they can apply the skill well. If it does not go to plan the student can usually answer why. The student now uses the skill in their general activity, but it is limited to specific situations. As a result the learner sees the limitations of the rules and starts to experiment with more generalised concepts of the skill. The performance is much more consistent and the outcome is achieved more often that not.

Cognitive: The student is using the skill as part of the activity and the overall structure is good. In applying the skill to varied settings the cognitive activity still remains high.

Bio-mechanical: The effort and movement is more often appropriate for the setting and reasonably smooth. The muscles are more in tune with the movements

Physiological: The speed and endurance is effected by small inconsistencies, but the overall efficiency is greatly improved and sessions can now be longer. A more relaxed style allows proprioception (Spatial awareness) to develop.

Skilled

The student can apply the skill if given the opportunity to plan ahead and can foresee common problems and avoid them. The student is associating past situations with current problems and making specific modifications to the skills through a process of self reflection (reflective practice). Rules have been replaced general principles. As a result the performance is consistent and the outcome is reached in all but the most technically demanding of situations.

Cognitive: The student understands the whole skill and its relationship to performance. The comprehension of the complex nature of the activity and the inappropriateness of strict rules. In order to reduce cognitive activity the student calls on previous experience to react rather then consider their next move.

Bio-mechanical: The student has a range of techniques for many different situations and can consistently call on these in their performance. New environments require extra thinking, but after an initial appraisal through trial and possible error, the new environment is quickly mastered. The student is also aware and able to determine ways of making the movement more efficient.

Physiological: The performance will require minimal effort and efficiency will be high. As such sessions can be longer as fatigue becomes less of an issue.

Skillful

The student can apply the skill on the go in demanding situations and adapt to use other techniques or models as appropriate. The student can perform the skill with autonomy and creativity. The ability to modify their actions to a wide variety of situations is possible because the student can extrapolate their experience based on their understanding of movement. Performance is fluid and decisions are made intuitively to refine and adapt to real time events. As such the outcome is nearly always achieved.

Cognitive: The student clearly understands the activity in much detail and most movements will be automatic, with only attention focused on the finest of motor control. The student will be aware of and respond to changes in the environment that may effect their performance and adjust accordingly. The individual will be applying strategic planning and tactics to their performance.

Bio-mechanical: The skill will appear smooth and at times effortless in a variety of environments. The student will be able to adapt and justify that change. As a result the student will constantly refine their performance to achieve maximum output from minimal input.

Physiological: The effort will be minimal and efficiency high. Muscles will have adapted to their activity and be able to maintain performance for extended periods without fatigue. Recovery will be quick.

Other Learning theories

There are several other theories that cover skill acquisition and learning from different stand points, I have highlighted a few here.

10 Year - 10000 hour rule

There are many suggestion that to reach the level of 'expert' in a sport or compete activity it takes 10 years or 10000 hours of deliberate practice. What this means is that to start off with to reach the highest level of skill across the whole gambit of individual skills that make up climbing, you need to be dedicated to the sport for 10 years of deliberate practice.

Where deliberate practice includes three major components that are regularly changed and followed throughout your climbing. Those components are:

- **Setting specific goals.**

- **Obtaining immediate feedback on performance.**

- **Concentrating on technique as much as outcome.**

It is potentially up to us the coaches to help students develop deliberate practice through our coaching. In doing so we can help our clients to help themselves in the long term.

Schmidt's Schema Theory

Again this is another theory and whilst not strictly aimed at the stages of learning, it may well be applicable in the later stages of learning. The theory suggest that every movement requires four pieces of information to be retrieved.

1. **The Initial Conditions -** Our Starting Point

2. **Certain aspects of the motor action -** How hard and fast we are going to move those muscle required.

3. **The result of the action -** Will we be successfully or fail

4. **The sensory consequences of the action -** Did it feel right, wrong, etc...

We can help more advanced learners by examining which of these areas was not correct in a specific movement, especially in complex boulder problems. Was the starting point correct, did the climber over or under estimate the power needed to perform that action, did the climber succeed. If they didn't succeed did they think they would be successful before or did they simply not believe the move was possible. Finally was the feeling of the action appropriate for what the climber actually did.

Bandurra's Social Learning Theory

Bandurra has found many psychological characteristics of learning and performance applying them to many different fields. This social learning theory was develop in 1961 and was researched through the study of children. As such it might be a better theory to apply to teaching younger climbers.

This theory has three main concepts:

- **People can learn through observation.**

- **Mental states are an essential part of learning.**

- **Learning will not necessarily result in a change of behaviour.**

In particular Bandurra found that children would mirror the behaviour they observed adults doing and that observational learning could come from a live model, a verbal description of the behaviour or a symbolic model of a real or fictional character through film, TV or other media.

What this says is that coaches working with groups of young people we need to lead by example. In doing so we can help our students mirror the behaviour we are exhibiting.

Curiosity and Learning

In 2009 the California Institute of Technology researched Curiosity as the wick that keeps the candle of learning burning. They showed that the level of curiosity was related to the retention of semantic information in laboratory tests. That included fMRI scans that showed the reward centre of the brain was more activated the higher the level of report curiosity.

Coaches can arguably utilise this by helping spark students curiosity when introducing semantic or technical information. In doing so we can aid retention of that information.

Fear based Conditioning

Whilst we cover fear and its effects on learning in the next chapter. Here we look at conditioned responses that are cause by a fearful stimuli. This conditioning is a evolutionary trait that evolved to help us learn to avoid hazards. It is caused by the process in the brain when we are exposed to a fearful stimuli like falling off we not only stimulate the adrenal system to cope with the threat but also the reward centres so we learn from these extreme situations.

In modern society and climbing this can lead to fear conditioning to inappropriate stimuli. Often it is these misaligned responses we need to deal with when trying to help a climber overcome fears when lead climbing. For example someone moving from Trad climbing where falling off is more often than not avoided at all costs, to Sport climbing where falling off is necessary to push yourself. Can mean people bring the same response of falling in trad climbing across to their sports climbing.

Positive Conditioning

This is one of the most primitive forms of learning theory that was first experimentally explored by Russian scientist Pavlov with dogs. His experiments looked at the uses of positive and negative conditioning to get a dog to learn that a sound means food. The result was that the dogs would eventually salivate when they heard the bell.

What we as coaches can take from this is that positive reinforcement is a key aspect of getting people to do what we want. As it is a basic psychological law that any behaviour which is rewarded or praised will become stronger.

As such it is extremely important to remember that when coaching rewarding good technique or tactics with a simple "That was great" or "Well done, that was fantastic" will help reinforce the behaviour.

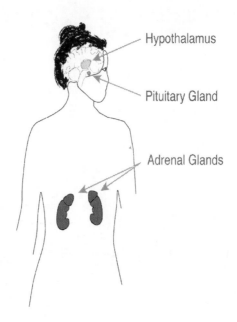

Hypothalamus

Pituitary Gland

Adrenal Glands

4 - Anxiety and Learning

Whilst many coaching environments are reasonably safe and comfortable, when coaching climbing we can put our students under much psychological pressure. This chapter deals with the theory and practice of the effects of anxiety on us and how that can disrupt students learning.

What is Anxiety

At is most simple, anxiety is simply worrying about things, as climbers we often experience these worrying thoughts as 'fear'. It goes deeper than just thoughts though. As those worries can cause a cascading of reaction of feelings and emotions that react throughout our bodies and give us real physiological symptoms. As such anxiety has two dimensions the worrying thoughts that are described as cognitive anxiety, as they exist only in our mind. The second dimension is the physical manifestations of the emotional response, this is referred to as somatic anxiety.

Both of these can be interpreted both positively and negatively. So whereas someone might thrive on nervous energy another person might be virtually paralysed by those same thoughts and feelings.

Fear and Anxiety are to a certain extent evolutionary relics that still effect us and are present in most mammals. It is often referred to as the 'flight or fight response' to stressful situations. Whilst most people understand that fear results in a dose of adrenalin, how and why that happens are often misunderstood, as are the effects.

Effectively a fearful thought, event or stimulus creates a chain reaction that feeds down through what is referred to as the HPA axis. In that fear stimulates the Hypothalamus, which in turn sends a hormone that is received by the Pituitary Gland. This in turn sends another hormone that is received by the adrenal gland that sits on top of the kidneys, which gives us a dose of adrenalin.

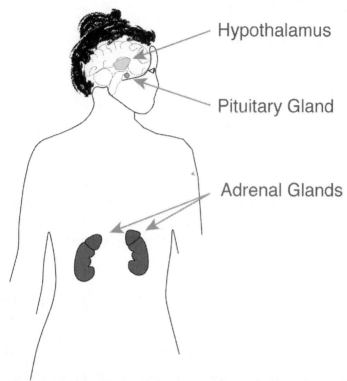

Hypothalamus

Pituitary Gland

Adrenal Glands

This (Hypothalamus-Pituitary-Adrenal) HPA Axis is also responsible for regulating digestion, the immune system, our moods, emotions, sexuality and energy management. Its trigger though is often seen as stress, which can come from a variety of sources.

A further effect of the fight or flight response is the focusing of attention. Evolutionary we needed to focus on a way out or a weakness in the opposition or situation we found ourselves in. In climbing this often means that we loose control over what we are focused on. Often people can become 'hold blind' as panic overcomes them and they stop focusing on technique and instead revert to a more primal survival instinct.

Cognitive Anxiety

This is the worrying thoughts that anyone can suffer from when being placed in new, novel or potentially dangerous settings. Often this can be a simple thought that starts to override our mind, like can I make this move, what will happen when I fall, I am a long way up and the ground looks far away.

Cognitive anxiety is the trigger for the physiological response. However as we will see later, the negative effects of anxiety, that can lead to performance drops have a relationship between this cognitive anxiety and somatic anxiety.

Typical manifestations of cognitive anxiety can be described as:

Indecision, sense of confusion, feeling heavy, negative thoughts, poor concentration, irritability, fear, forgetfulness, loss of confidence, images of failure, defeatist self-talk, feeling rushed, feeling weak, constant dissatisfaction, unable to take instructions and thoughts of avoidance

Somatic Anxiety

As we have already discussed the somatic anxiety is the bodies physiological response to stress. It is the bodies way to ready us in evolutionary terms to fight for survival or run for our life. Whilst we have seen how that response is triggered, what we haven't seen is how that effects us physiologically. In terms of how we are getting ready for this a fight or flight to the death, which takes on new meanings in climbing. So what is going on inside us that would make a difference to survival?

The initial reaction of adrenalin is to increase both our breathing and heart rate, not only in terms of beats or breathes per minute, but it also increases the volume of blood we pump and air that we breathe, with each heart beat or breath. This is often referred to as tidal volume.

As we mentioned the HPA axis also controls digestion and energy resources. Adrenal response helps divert energy away from digestive system and shunts it towards skeletal muscle, priming the body for action.

All of these and a few more effects give distinct symptoms that are listed below. You might notice that you have experienced them either prior to or during a climb. You may also have experienced them in particularly stressful situation like public speaking and prior to an exam, interview or assessment.

The symptoms of somatic anxiety are:

Increased blood pressure, pounding heart, increased respiration rate, sweating, clammy hands and feet, butterflies in the stomach, adrenaline surge, dry mouth, need to urinate, muscular tension, tightness in neck and shoulders, trembling, feeling jittery, incessant talking, blushing, pacing up and down, distorted vision, loss of peripheral vision, twitching, yawning, voice distortion, nausea, vomiting, diarrhea, loss of appetite, sleeplessness and loss of libido.

Behavioural Effects of Anxiety

Whilst anxiety effects us both mentally and physically through cognitive and somatic pathways. Those effects can change our behaviour and again these effects can be seen as:

Biting fingernails, lethargic movements, inhibited posture, playing safe, going through the motions, introversion, uncharacteristic displays of extroversion, fidgeting, wiping sweaty palms, avoidance of eye contact and covering face with hand.

As coaches, noticing these behavioural effects can be the first signs that our clients are being effected by anxiety. However it is important that not only can we notice these effects, but understand and at times preempt situations which will unduly stress clients, as it can effect their ability to learning.

What Makes us anxious?

There are many things that makes an individual nervous or anxious. However in general there are things we need to recognise as a coach that we can almost immediately assume that someone will be under the influence of anxiety.

To start with the first time you meet a client, both you and they will probably experience some kind of anxiety, as there is a degree of uncertainty and worry about meeting someone for the first time. If you like that first meeting can be the typical 'first day' nerves and similar to the first time at a new school, college, university or job.

When we introduce a new skill there are often doubts in the students mind as to whether they are capable of achieving this new skill. The same can be true of new crags or environments. So the first time someone is on 'real' rock rather than at an indoor wall. The first time you take a client to the top of single pitch crag. The clients first multi-pitched climb or even the first time at a cliff that is new to them and of course their first real lead climb. All of these will undoubtedly induce anxiety.

What is important is that we as coaches understand this and do something to manage that potential anxiety, often through progressive teaching. This is important because failure to do so can have a catastrophic effect on a students performance and ability to learn, as anxiety has a direct link to learning through a variety of models and theories that have linked performance with anxiety.

Performance - Anxiety Theories

There are number theories that have linked anxiety and performance. It is a much researched field as the ability to perform to the best of a sport persons ability during highly stressful competitive settings, mean that many top athletes have needed to form strategies to overcome the effects of anxiety on their performance.

As such sports psychologist have looked at a variety of ways to theorise exactly what happens to us under high stress conditions versus low stress. In two of these theories the researchers actually used climbing as a vehicle to research the wider field of performance anxiety.

Here we will look at several of these theories and again some are not current thinking, but can be used to simplify the understanding for both coaches and athletes.

Multidimensional Anxiety Theory (MAT)

This theory was first put forward by Yerkes and Dobson, in 1908 and they described a law of performance versus somatic anxiety. Where if plotted on a graph you got an inverted U shape, at one end the low anxiety state was related to lower levels of performance, as anxiety increases the performance also increases to a point know as optimum arousal and performance. If anxiety continued to rise then the performance started to drop off.

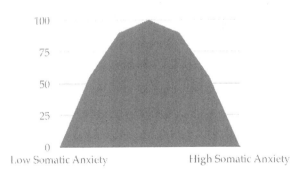

Low Somatic Anxiety   High Somatic Anxiety

However this only took into account somatic anxiety and not cognitive arousal and often this is a simple line of a graph, where as cognitive arousal increases performance decreases. As such whilst these hypothesis stand true in isolation, anxiety is often the interaction of both cognitive and somatic anxiety.

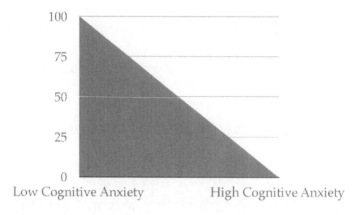

100
75
50
25
0

Low Cognitive Anxiety   High Cognitive Anxiety

CUSP Catastrophe Model

The CUSP catastrophe model comes from mathematical models where a small change in a system with two variables leads to a big change in the output of that system. It was applied to the sporting anxiety theories in 1987 by Hardy and Fazey, who suggested that cognitive and somatic anxiety do indeed interact to create performance 'catastrophes'. In essence they combined the stand alone graphs of Yerkes and Dobson Theory into a 3-Dimensional Model.

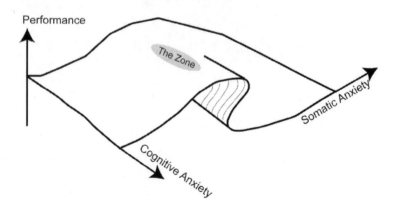

Here they proposed that like the MAT theory, somatic anxiety did give and inverted U shape, when someone was under low levels of cognitive anxiety. However if cognitive anxiety is higher, this can lead to a sudden drop off in performance, the model when plotted looks like the crest of a breaking wave.

In this theory they managed to explain why in certain situations sportsman and women have suffered massive performance drops. It is also used to explain the area in which both cognitive and somatic arousal reach their optimum levels for an athlete to enter 'The Zone', where performance is at its maximum. Although it failed to answer what the underlying processes that lead to those drops. If you like it showed the how and when, but not why. The next three theories have attempted to explain why we see this performance drop in highly stressful situations.

Ironic Effects

This was first put forward in 1992 by Wegner who designed an experiment that looked at repression, suppression and thought. His classic experiment was to ask participants to not think about a white polar bear for a certain period of time and to press a counter every time they did, this was repressing the thought. They showed that this trying not to think about something, actually causes the thought to occur more and to a certain extent people became obsessed with that thought.

He then tried to get them to not think about the white polar bear, by thinking instead of a red VW Beatle, this is classically seen as suppressing the thought by giving someone an object or idea to replace it. This proved relatively useful in trying to remove the obsessive nature of a thought that you want people not to think about.

It is only applicable to extreme sports, if a climber or athlete has a negative self-talk theme that may be part of of the cognitive aspect of anxiety. In that they might try to repress thoughts, like 'Don't fall' and rather than trying to not think about the words 'Don't Fall', we might get them to replace the idea with a new thought like, 'I am strong'. It did not however manage to answer the question of what goes on to produce performance drops.

Conscious Processing

Originally developed by Master's in 1992 and subsequently tested and supported by several experiments. One by Pijper in 2003, who used climbing to support the theory. In the Pijper's experiment they had climbers traverse two near identical boulder problems that traversed a wall. One low to the ground and one at height.

They found that the length of time, the number of moves, the number of wrong moves and hesitation all increased with height. Leading them to support the notion that the added anxiety of height increased thought, making people revert from more autonomous performance to more consciously thinking about every move.

The theory also suggests that depending on how people have learnt and their level of skill (i.e. are they an expert), meant that there were potentially differ-ent effects. We shall look at these at the end of this chapter when we examine at implicit versus explicit learning.

Essentially conscious processing suggests that an expert can revert to more conscious thought when under high levels of anxiety. In essence this can be seen as someone reverting back to being a begin-ner as they have to consciously think through every move. It is this reverting to conscious rather than autonomous processing that results in performance catastrophes

Processing Efficiency Theory

Processing Efficiency Theory was first put forward my Eyseck and Calvo in 1992 and subsequently sup-ported in research by Hardy and Hutchinson (2007), who again used climbing as a vehicle to test the hy-pothesis. In the research they got climbers to climb routes at or near their limit, in high and low anxiety states (Lead climbing and on top rope). They meas-ured both cognitive and somatic anxiety.

The theory that it supported is best seen as visual-ising the human brain as a computer, like we did in the last chapter, where working memory has that limit of 7+/-2 chunks of information. Just like a computer, where if we open too many windows or applications, the processor starts to struggle, slow down and at times crashes, the same holds true of performance.

Process efficiency theory suggests that a reduction in the ability of our working memory to cope under the greater cognitive loads caused by anxiety. As those 7+/-2 spaces for processing are taken over by worrying thoughts and the effects of anxiety, we lose the ability to perform as efficiently as we can when not overly stressed. To counteract this drop in efficiency we initially increase the effort we put in, however as we continue to load the system with stress then we eventually fail, often before we would have if we were relaxed because we are trying harder.

Anxiety's Effect on Learning

From these few models into anxiety and its effects we can see that learning can potentially be effected in two ways. First we shall look at how anxiety can effect our students short-term memory by reducing its capacity and secondly we shall explore what the findings of conscious process have through implicit and explicit learning. Before finally questioning what we can do as a coach or instructor to reduce the negative effects of anxiety on learning.

What Happen to that 7+/-2 chunks of information

The first and most important way that anxiety can effect learning is through our working memory, as processing efficiency predicts that as we become more and more stressed, the ability of our minds to process information reduces. Thus it is quite sensible, although there is as yet no empirical evidence to suggest that those 7+/-2 chunks of information that we can use to process information when learning can start to be reduced, the connection is strong.

As such the ability for a student to process a lot of information starts to become impaired and the point at which they become overloaded can be greatly reduced.

Implicit vs Explicit Learning

Conscious processing also makes a suggestion that how we learn can effect how our performance can be disrupted by anxiety. This time it is more aimed at experts or people who are a reasonable way along in terms of their stage of learning. Before we look at this, we must first describe to you what we mean by implicit versus explicit learning.

Explicit learning is learning that has occurred via a set of direct instructions as to how to achieve something, in that the coach may well have given a strict recipe that if followed results in a skill being learnt. The rules are explicitly and consciously known to the learner. Even if not directly given by the coach, a student can still formulate there own set of explicit rules.

Implicit learning, is more a form of self coaching or guided discovery, where a set recipe for a technique is not necessarily presented or indeed developed independently by the the student. Implicit learning then is more the automatic approach to a skill.

What is argued in the conscious processing hypothesis is that someone who has learnt to be an expert under more explicit instruction, when stressed is more likely to revert back to consciously processing every movement. Just like a beginner has to do when learning a skill.

One of the keys to this then can be allowing the students to learn through guided discovery. However even then the student may well develop their own set of rules. As such this is a tricky aspect of coaching to address. Having got a student into the ball park of a skill, we then need to help them break those rules and use instinct rather than a recipe.

How we do this may require getting the student to climb quickly or completing a skill without giving them time to think it through. In essence we are trying to get the student to climb on instinctive reaction, rather than conscious thought. As such it is another layer to add to our coaching and is best suited to people who are well along the stages of learning and it will take a long time for a student to develop these skills.

Controlling Anxiety

This is often done in a variety of ways, in that the client is the centre of a model that looks at the environment in which we are coaching (venue and weather), the aim of that day and what tasks you set. All of these interact with each other and if we consider what we can change or can't. Then as a coach we can instantly start to consider how we can manage and adapt our lesson for coaching a variety of individuals.

Firstly it is impossible to change the client at the centre of the model, but we can adapt to our clients needs, level of learning and how well adapted they are to the stresses we can place them under coaching a high risk sport like climbing.

Similarly we can't change the weather, but as a result of it we can change the environment in which we are coaching. Often this needs to be chosen carefully at the beginning of the day, based on the aim, weather and tasks. Is your venue too high, too exposed, too hot or too cold? Are the routes too steep, slabby, easy or difficult for the client. This and a whole variety of considerations can make the selecting a venue, a route or even what pitch each client gets an incredibly important decision for the clients learning. By careful selection we can reduce the level of anxiety and can increase a students ability to learn.

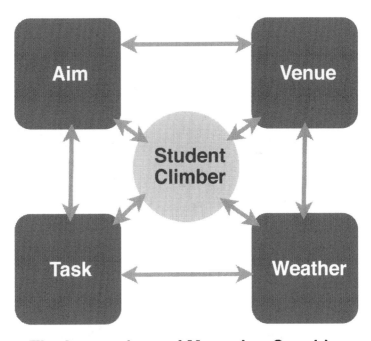

The Interactions of Managing Coaching
To control anxiety we can change the aim, task (venue, but not the weather or the student

Hand in hand with venue selection, we can also to a certain extent change the aim of a session, based on the clients ability. So as an example a client wants to learn to lead, do you put them on lead first or do you spend time teaching them all the components of leading (climbing, belaying from the top of a pitch, placing runners, making belays, etc...) before bringing those skills together? By doing this, we can help a student develop the chunks or building blocks of a bigger skill by tailoring a session to just those chunks rather than the whole skill. If they have these skills chunked they will be under less cognitive load and they can therefore cope with a bit more anxiety.

Finally and we will cover this more in the advanced coaching session, when we look closely at us the coach. Are you the best person for the job or can you as a coach decide that another coach professional has a certain skillset that you do not currently possess and refer the client on or call in assistance. Similar as we shall see in the advanced coaching chapter, there can be issues with coach-athlete relationships, maybe you make them nervous or vice-versa.

Mental Skills for Anxiety Control

As well as our direct choices and behaviour, we can also employ mental skills to help clients manage their anxiety. This is covered in much more detail in the Effective Coaching: Mental Skill for Climbing Coaches. In the context of this book, we are going to explore relaxation.

The reasons for this is that relaxation is a very effective tool to combat anxiety, as it not only helps to relax the mind, but more importantly it counteracts the physiological symptoms of adrenalin. In essence we are trying to get students to remain relaxed when climbing. Often when lead climbing, the relaxed state is lost when anxiety takes over.

To start with, being and staying relaxed as a coach is imperative, as we can effect the students if we appear nervous or anxious. As such the clients can and will mirror our behaviour. So if we can stay relaxed and talk calmly to our clients then we can utilise this mirroring effect.

Secondly we can introduce relaxation to the climber on the ground before they head off on a lead. You will need to sit the client down and introduce them to slow and controlled breathing. So get them to copy you as you take a slow inhalation through the nose, breathing in for 4-8 seconds, followed by a slow and steady exhalation through mouth, often having the lips only slightly open help this, so its like they are breathing out through a straw.

Once they have mastered that you can add a mantra like 're-lax' so on the inhalation get them to think 're' and on the exhalation 'lax'.

Again this is not something they will master in five minutes, but something which if practiced daily for 10 minutes will result in them being able to relax in a matter of seconds, after around 2 to 4 weeks of practice.

Manipulating Anxiety

It sounds very ethically dubious to manipulate people emotions which is essentially what anxiety is. However there is a growing undercurrent of research that shows that if we can habituate people to anxiety they can 'learn' how to cope with it.

This has been shown in tests where a training regime followed by a test or examine has resulted in a dip in performance. In more recent test where a they have manipulated anxiety in the training phases the performance decrement has been less.

What these recent test has shown is that it is important to get people into the ball park of a skill before we manipulate anxiety. So in simple terms make sure people can clip a quickdraw with a simulated lead line before you get them to lead properly. Basically don't do this with beginners and novices, but for climbers leading or competing it is an important thing to consider.

So how can we manipulate people anxiety?

Essentially we have to look to what people fear and create an environment where we can gradually ramp up anxiety.

- **Isolation** - Moving someone to an isolated area prior to setting a task

- **Performing in front of a group** - Getting peers or on lookers to cheer and/or boo

- **Add time constraints** - Get a stopwatch out, but beware speed often leads to greater drops in performance.

- **Turning a training into a mini competition** - using new problems as a competition

- **Put people on the lead** - Perhaps the easiest way to increase anxiety.

- **Lying about grade** - telling people they are on a harder route than it actually is.

- **Videoing people** - This can work along side ambarrassing people, by telling them you are going to post the video on Youtube. My advice is don't carry the threat through.

- **Embarrassing people** - by telling them you are going to post results publically.

All of these should be seen as threats to manipulate peoples emotions and should be used sparingly in the run up to a competition. If you use them then afterwards explain why and how you used them and what the point of being underhand was. This is important, as in manipulating our clients we are in a dangerous area of breaking the trust that develops between a coach and their client.

Once you have created fear in your students it is important to chat about how it effect them so try and tease out the somatic and cognitive effects on them and how it may have effected there performance and how they control it and to a certain extent ignore aspects of it as a natural response.

Summary

Hopefully you now understand what anxiety is, how it effects us mentally and physically. On top of this what that anxiety can do to an individuals performance and also how it can effect their learning. We have also touched on the subject of controlling the effects of anxiety.

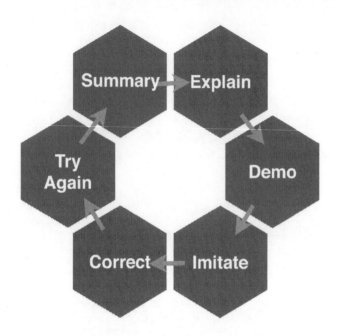

5 - Teaching Models

So far we have examined how we learn a new skill. This chapter now looks at applying that understanding of learning to our teaching. We move from basic models to more complex ones, finally look at the individual building blocks of those models in greater depth and how they fit in with the stages of learning.

What do we know about learning?

So far we have looked at the basic psychological principles of how people learn and process information. We have examined how that can be effected through the stages of learning and anxiety. So now we are going to reverse that based on those underlying fundamental principles of learning and suggest that there are several ways in which we can apply this to teaching or coaching of any skill.

That skill could be a bio-mechanical one like belaying, it could be a more physiological one like how to develop strength or endurance or it could be a psychological one like reading a route or remaining calm on lead. Whatever the skill these principals can be applied to learning it.

There are numerous basic models of coaching and teaching, all of which have pro's and con's. After introducing you to a couple of the more common models we shall then go onto suggest that within them all are several underlying ingredients. As long as you include those ingredients, the order in which you use them becomes less important than the fact that you included them.

Basic Teaching/Coaching Models

Just as in our learning models, the most basic was a 3 stage model of PLAN - DO - REVIEW the same is true of coaching. We need to plan a lesson or activity, get our students to do it and then get our students and ourselves to review it.

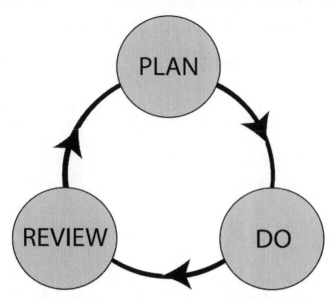

Like with learning this is a simplistic model and one that excludes some very important points. But if we look back at the accelerated learning cycle on page 15 and think about where we the coach can enhance the learning potential, in particular engaging with prior learning it too fits into a coaching model.

IDEAS model

The IDEAS model is an acronym, standing for:

Introduction

Demonstration

Explanation

Activity

Summary

It is one of the most simple of the coaching models. We shall explore the individual parts later, however for now its serves as an example of the simplest and often most taught basic teaching model. Its flaw is that only one part is focused on the student in the form of activity, and there is no taking into account you looking at there performance and trying to rectify it in some way.

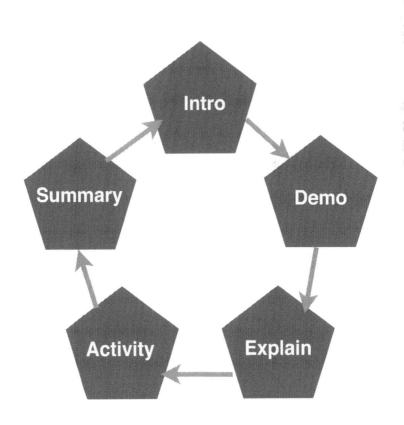

EDICTS Model

The EDICTS model is a much better coaching model, as it has more student centre aspects and it allows for observation, analysis and correcting mistakes. The EDICTS is another acronym, and stands for:

Explanation

Demonstration

Imitation

Corrections

Try again

Summary

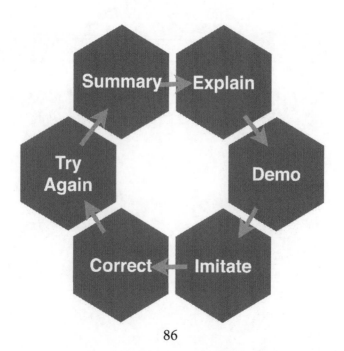

Again I don't want to go into great detail about these parts in this section as I will cover each important aspect of these models in depth in the next part of this chapter.

WAFSP Model

Again this is another cyclical model, that starts from the outset as a student centred approach by first watching someone perform before even setting a task. As such it is just another way of arranging some key ingredients. Again more aspects are student focused than other models, but it requires the students' spontaneous action. As such it is not suited to total novices.

Watch

Analyse

Feedback

Set task

Perform

Gagne's Nine Events of Instruction

Again this is yet another model of 'instructing' and follows more the accelerated learning cycle. However there are parts of the model that may well help us improve our coaching. As a model it is widely used in america on Wilderness Education Association and Outward Bound schemes, it is more aimed at classroom or outdoor teaching of groups of people. As such it is included as a model for completeness and to offer a wider base to our knowledge. I have also described the elements in order here, as there are differences to the major components of the preferable IDEAS, EDICT and WAFSP models. The nine stages are:

1. Gain the students Attention

2. Inform the learner of objectives

3. Stimulate the recall of prior learning

4. Present Stimulus Material

5. Provide learner guidance

6. Elicit Performance

7. Provide Feedback

8. Assess Performance

9. Enhance retention and transfer

Each of these stages then has a reason why it should happen, an aim and ways to achieve it.

Gaining Attention

AIM: To activate receptors in the brain, and focus them on you.

WHY: In order for any learning to take place, you must first capture the attention of the student.

HOW: A multimedia program with sound effects or music startles the senses with auditory or visual stimuli. An even better way to capture students' attention is to start each lesson with a thought-provoking question or interesting fact. Curiosity motivates students to learn.

Inform learners of objectives

AIM: to create a level of expectation for learning

WHY: Early in each lesson students should encounter a list of learning objectives. This initiates the internal process of expectancy and helps motivate the learner to complete the lesson.

HOW: Typically, learning objectives are presented in the form of "Upon completing this lesson you will be able to. . . ."

Stimulate recall of prior learning

AIM: To engage the retrieval and activation of short-term memory

WHY: Associating new information with prior knowledge can facilitate the learning process. It is easier for learners to encode and store information in long-term memory when there are links to personal experience and knowledge.

HOW: A simple way to stimulate recall is to ask questions about previous experiences and understanding of previous concepts or a body of content.

Present the content (Stimulus Material)

AIM: To allow perception of content

WHY: This event of instruction is where the new content is actually presented to the learner.

HOW: Content should be chunked and organized meaningfully and typically is explained and then demonstrated. To appeal to different learning modalities, a variety of media should be used if possible, including text, graphics, audio narration and video.

Provide "learning guidance"

AIM: To help learners encode information for long-term storage, additional guidance should be provided along with the presentation of new content.

HOW: Guidance strategies include the use of examples, non-examples, case studies, graphical representations, mnemonics and analogies.

Elicit performance (practice)

AIM: In this event of instruction, the learner is required to practice the new skill or behaviour.

WHY: Eliciting performance provides an opportunity for learners to confirm their correct understanding and the repetition further increases the likelihood of retention.

HOW: See section later on Effective Practice

Provide feedback

AIM: Reinforcement and assessment of correct performance

WHY: As learners practice new behavior it is important to provide specific and immediate feedback of their performance. Unlike questions in a post-test, exercises within tutorials should be used for comprehension and encoding purposes, not for formal scoring.

HOW: Guidance and answering Questions. This stage are called formative feedback. In that it helps the learn form the skill.

Assess Performance

AIM: To assess learning outcome

WHY: In order to see if your transfer of knowledge has resulted in learning

HOW: Observation of desired behaviour, Questioning or more formal written assessment. This is often referred to as summative assessment as it is a way to check the learner has acquired the skill.

Enhance Retention and Transfer

AIM: Encourage the use and application of learning.

WHY: It can help the students start to apply their new knowledge and skills outside the context of the course

HOW: Give students a meaningful context in which to apply this new knowledge.

Teachable Moments

Teachable moments are a great additional tool for coaching and is a technique that can have powerful results as it comes about through chance or occasionally through planning. Where you might know that you are going to come across a new or novel problem to the students.

An example of this might be when coaching climbing outside and rather than teach you students to abseil, you wait until the opportunity arises. When you either reach the top of the route and it is appropriate to abseil off or you know the weather is going to force a retreat at some point during the day and you utilise that opportunity to cover the skill of abseiling.

As such these teachable moments can occur naturally as situations develop or by careful planning. Where teaching that skill is done in context of where it would be used in a students climbing.

Curiosity and teaching

A bit like the teachable moments, these situations can occur naturally or through careful panning and their application to learning has only recently been unearthed by researchers at California Institute of Technology in 2009. In a series of experiments they showed that the more curious a person was the more they activated both the learning parts of the brain and the reward centre was. They also showed that greater levels of curiosity resulted in better retention of semantic information.

As such if we can raise someone's curiosity during a session, then that person is much more likely to not only retain that information but also get an intrinsic reward from gaining that information. As coaches we can frame a session for people who have already started to learn a skill by posing thought provoking questions. The students can answer the question by carrying out the lesson you have planned.

The Key Ingredients to Coaching Models

What follows are the building blocks of the IDEAS, EDICTS and WASFP coaching models. Exploring each facet in greater depth, explaining what they are and how we can use them most effectively in coaching to produce a skilful performance.

We focused on introducing a new skill, demonstrating that skill, explaining that skill, setting up some form of effective practice, observing and analysing that practice, before giving appropriate feedback and finally giving a conclusion to the session. Whilst presented here in that order, it is important to realise that to a certain extent that order is not set in stone. By presenting them in a different order and recycling components you can produce much stronger learning experiences for your students. However to start with using the IDEAS, EDICTS or WASFP model will help you develop the fundamental skills of coaching when it comes to skill acquisition.

Introduction

It goes without saying that coaching interactions have a beginning middle and an end. The introduction whether it be to a whole course, a session or an activity are often the springboard for setting up a good session. They are referred to in these models as introductions or explanations.

In terms of a course or day they are a great opportunity to introduce yourself to the group, but also potentially have the group introduce themselves to you and each other. Often asking the group their previous experience will help you to gauge there level of performance.

In terms of an individual session, the introduction is there to provide the framing of the activity and the context in which the skill being taught can be used. As such it is about putting what you are about to do into the bigger picture. Similarly are there any related skills that the students already have that can be brought to their attention, linking this new skill to lessons already learnt.

Where possible the introduction should be concise and succinct, mainly due to that magic number 7+/-2 as when we introduce a skill we can often throw too much information at our students.

As a guide think of the four **W**'s,

What are we going to do, What related skills do the students alreasdy have?

Why are we doing it

When can the skills be used? i.e. The context

Where its going to take place.

These are the overview of the activity and are separate from an explanation of an individual skill.

Demonstration

This is probably one of the most important aspects of coaching, many people learn through a variety of pathways, however seeing a whole and complete skill performed in real time, without any distractions like talking over it, gives people a picture in their head of what exactly they are trying to achieve.

This demonstration needs to be done in a place where everybody can see it. When everyone is paying attention. It should be done in real time and in a contextual setting where appropriate. An example would be a rock-over should be demonstrated on slab, rather than on an overhanging wall.

Once you have given a silent demonstration then there are several ways to add to this. One is to add an explanation whilst re-demonstrating it, the other is to get a group or individuals to talk you through what they just saw. The second way makes the group think more and you can add any points you think are important aspects of the skill. The second methods helps you confirm that the group were paying attention to the first example.

Explanation of a Skill

Again just like the introduction, the important thing to remember in an explanation of a skill is to keep it as brief as possible, as if combined with the demonstration, we can overload our students quite quickly. Remember the limit of 7±2 chunks of information. As mentioned in the demonstration part, it can be more effective to get the group to explain what they have just seen. This way more of the session is focused on them doing something.

Effective Practice

This is referred to in the activity, action, imitation or performing parts of the coaching models. It is the part in which the students undertake the skills you are trying to teach them. We have called it effective practice because how and why we set up that practice has many considerations and in choosing the right type of practice environment we can help make learning more effective.

First of all, is the environment right for the learner, are the problems you set too hard or too easy? Do the students have any pre-existing skills to call upon to help them achieve the goal set for the session.

The next thing to consider is what type of practice we are going to use. As each type has different pro's and con's associated with it and often the choice depends upon our perception as a coach to what stage of learning an individual or a group is at, as well as the complexity of the skill.

Types of Practice

There are many types of practice we can set up. These are:

- **Blocked** – repeating an exercise over and over. (1,1,1,1,1.......)

- **Series** – repeating different exercise in order. (1,1,1,1,2,2,2,2,...)

- **Varied** – repeating different exercises. (1,2,3,4,1,2,3,4....)

- **Random** – repeating exercises in random order. (1,4,2,3,3,1,2,4,1,)

- **Bilateral** – repeating the exercise left and right handed, up and down or in both directions.

- **Augmented** – having a rest/distractor tasks in between practice.

- **Grouped practice** – extra information gained through observation.

- **Whole-part-whole** - Breaking a complex skill into parts before putting back together again.

Blocked Practice

This is the simplest form of practice, in that we get the student to repeat the skill over and over again. It is very effective at getting people to start learning a technique and get them into the ball park of what we want them to achieve. However if we want someone to utilise that technique in a skillful setting then we need to change how we set up practice.

Remember the throwing a ball into a bucket exercise from earlier, I give you 10 balls and you throw them underarm one by one into the bucket, you very quickly learn the movement to achieve the task but will probably only be good at throwing the balls underarm from that one position. We very quickly get the learner into the 'ball park' of what we are trying to achieve, but have just taught them a technique and not a skill.

As such blocked practice is good for beginners but not for people who already have the start of the technique we are trying to turn into a skill. As the movement program only remains in short term memory and is less likely to be move back and forth to the long term memory. In climbing teaching belaying is a good example of blocked practice, when someone is learning to belay for the first time they end up repeating the movement over and over until the person reaches the top.

Series Practice

This is where we might set two or more exercises and repeat each one for a number of tries. If we take the ball throwing exercise again, we might get the person to throw, 5 underarm throws from 5 metres, 5 overarm throws from 5 metres, 5 underarm throws from 8m and 5 overarm throws from 8 metres.

Here we have 4 different sets of practice, each one slightly different. We would get the learner to repeat the each exercise a set number of times before moving onto the next exercise(1,1,1,2,2,2,3,3,3,4,4,4). As such each time we change the exercise from one to another we are having to send and retrieve information from our short term memory to long term memory, as such more learning is likely to occur, due to the movement program not just being repeated in short-term memory.

Again this is more suited to the early stages of learning, although we are now starting to turn that isolated technique into a skill.

Varied Practice

This is similar to series practice, although rather than have multiple attempts at each exercise we only now have one go at each working through each permutation of the exercise in a regular order (1,2,3,4,1,2,3,4,etc...). Again this further adds to the sending and retrieving of information from long term to short term memory.

In terms of our throwing example then, we would get the student to throw one ball underarm from 5 metres, one ball overarm from 5 metres, one ball underarm from 8 metres and one ball overarm from 8 metres, and repeat that 5 times.

Again this is more suitable for learners who already have the basic techniques and who are developing putting that technique into a more skillful setting.

Random Practice

At its most simple this is reordering a finite set of exercises into a random order. With the coach changing the order of presentation as they see fit. What this does is stop the student preempting what they are about to do and instead make them start to access that movement program from there long term memory without prior warning.

This form of practice is better suited to people in the mid to later stages of learning, as they already have the technique and are starting to show that they can apply it to a more skillful setting.

In our throwing example then it would be driven by the coach, alternating the distance of 5 or 8 metres at random and whether the student is to throw the ball overarm or under just before the student throws the ball. In essence we are trying to keep the student on their toes and force them to retrieve information from long-term memory to short-term memory and back again.

However there is another way that we can arrange random practice, in that we can alter the task entirely, so in the case of the ball throwing, we could start moving the student to a random distance from the bucket, as well as still utilising the underarm/overarm throws.

In climbing then this might be seen as getting a student to climb a few different boulder problems. After they have achieved the problem you can highlight a random hold that they can no longer use, forcing them to rethink the problem each time.

Bi-lateral Practice

Most people in the world have one dominant hand, in that they are left or right handed. However in most climbing situations you need to be ambidextrous or just be able to use your non-dominant hand when necessary.

Staying with our ball and bucket example, we could have added left and right handed throws from the beginning of our practice from blocked, series, random and varied. Bilateral practice allows a certain amount of cross over and refinement of motor skills from the left and right handed programs.

In climbing this could mean you get people to traverse both left and right or climb up and down a problem. Belaying you can even get people to belay a top-rope climber up and then get them to reverse down whilst the belayer reverses the belaying pattern. A further exercise is get them to belay in there non-dominant hand, something that is required on many multipitch stances outside.

What this is aimed at doing is developing a more robust skills that is more easily adaptable and applicable to new settings. This technique can be used to help move people through the stages of learning and whilst it can be used in the initial stages, it is often best introduced after the students are in the ball park of what you want them to achieve.

Augmented Practice

As we have discussed with other types of practice, at times we want the learner to send and retrieve information from long term to short term memory. We can achieve this through blocked, random and varied practice. However we can also deliberately add some down time from an activity or a distractor task.

Again turning to the ball and bucket task, we can get someone to practice for a certain amount of time using series, blocked, varied, bi-lateral or random techniques, but get them to do something else in between these practices. For example we could add a totally new and different task of getting them to try and throw the ball over their shoulder and catch it behind their back.

Their attention has now changed to this new skill and in trying to focus on it and learn they essentially forget about the old task for a short while. When they return to the ball and bucket task they are force into retrieving and reconstructing that program from long term memory.

In climbing when teaching belaying we can have someone belay, and after go onto to climb whilst someone else belays. This effectively augments the practice, similarly, if you see that someone has really started to pick up a skill, you can move the session onto something totally different for a period of time before returning back to that previous skill. As such augmented practice is more suited to people who have started to develop a technique into a skill and is about deliberate disrupting learning so you force them to use their long-term memory.

Grouped Practice - Observational Learning

Grouped practice is the using of a two or more people in a practice situation. Where each person takes it in turns to practice using one of the practice regimes mentioned here. However in having only one person do the skill whilst the others are watching we are giving each person additional information from the observation of others performing the skill.

This observational learning if you like gives more visual feedback to the individual learner and that feedback is often processed internally by the learner. In studies this has been shown to help increase the speed at which a skill is learnt and can be utilised at any stage of learning.

So in the case of the ball throwing example we would have one person complete each set of practice, whilst one or more looked on.

In belaying we can have a rotation of three or more people, where one person climbs, another belays and the others back up the belayer whilst observing.

Whole - Part - Whole Practice

If we are introducing a totally new skill to someone, a skill that is extremely complex then getting them to try and replicate the whole technique is simply not going to work. Instead we break that skill down into smaller more attainable chunks and get our students to learn these before putting it all together.

This can be effective when starting out because of that 7+/-2 chunks of information being too small for the complete skill to be taught at once. This limit is a good gauge to when a skill should be broken down or not. Then we as the coach define the chunks we want them to learn before we can put them together.

There are a few caveats to this type of practice, the first is when introducing the skill, it is best to show the skill as a whole. This way the learners can see what the end picture is. Then we can get them to practice the parts of the skill, before bringing it all together at the end. Hence the name Whole-Part-Whole.

The second caveat, is that people who are already highly skilled in a sport or technique may well be more able to simply work on the whole from the start. Rather than breaking the skill down into is constituent parts and putting back together. This has some cross over to the argument about implicit and explicit learning, by breaking the technique down for an expert we are in essence giving them some explicit instructions rather than relying on implicit learning. As such under high anxiety situations the learner may be more likely to revert back to those building blocks rather than complete the skill as one flowing motion.

A dyno or dynamic bouldering moves are good examples of skills that are complex as they have a beginning, middle and end. The set up, the launch and the catching of the next hold. As such breaking it into these chunks can accelerate the acquisition of this skill.

Reducing the degree's of Freedom of a Task

A bit like the whole-part-whole approach, but it may be done for a variety of less complex skills and can help get students into the ball park of a skill.

In essence we are trying to eliminate the number of variables a student has to deal with to complete skill. This can be done by making a task as simple as possible.

A great example of this would be when teaching climbers to use a clove hitch to tie into a belay. To start with you might introduce one point to attach to and get the climber to practice tying into this point and adjusting the length and tension. The next step might be to introduce a different way to tie into one point (in reach and out of reach). Finally you can add a second point, by which point the student has had success with the easier single point belay before moving onto the two points.

Another example might be not allowing the climber to use hands when they are rocking over on an easy slab, as it stops them using the hands and instead just focus on balance.

Correcting Performance - Observation, Analysis and Feedback

In the various models this is referred to as correcting, analyzing, watching and giving feedback. In essence then there are three important things that happen when we are trying to correct performance. First of all we need to watch a student performance and based on this observation we then analyze their performance before deciding how we can give feedback to them to improve.

As you can see you cannot have one without the other aspects, as such we have grouped all three of these aspects of the coaching model together.

Observation

There are numerous ways we can observe performance in a modern world, as well as viewing people in 'real time' with our eyes, we can also video people with a camcorder, camera, smart phone or tablet. To start with we are going to look at just observations in real time.

Real Time Observations

Whilst we have already mentioned our eyes, there is much more information we can gain from observing performance than simply watching someone. We can listen to them and whilst we can't feel them climb we can ask them how something felt, although we need to use this cautiously.

The simplest form of observation then is visual, but there are many aspects to it that need to be considered to make best use of this simple yet powerful coaching tool.

The first thing to decide is where are you going to observe from, in an indoor setting this tends to be from the ground, but we can change our perspective from directly behind the climber to looking across the wall. Dependent on what you are teaching and looking for this needs to alter. Similarly, it may take both perspectives to observe a performance.

After the perspective that you choose, you also need to consider whether what you saw was a one off mistake or something the climber is doing repeatedly. As such you might have to allow the students some time to practice before you jump to conclusions from a one off observation.

At the same time as watching someone we can also listen to them, are they grunting or showing signs of excessive effort? Can you hear their feet touch the wall?

Real time observation is best suited to people in the early to mid stages of learning, as the mistakes are often bigger and much easier to identify. However this may be effected by your experience as a coach or instructor as you develop an eye for common mistakes.

Video Observation

We can also aid our real time observations with the use video recording equipment. The use of smart phones or tablet computers are ideal for this, as they can record and playback instantly. There use needs to be considered though, as many people simply don't like being filmed and will suffer from performance drops due to anxiety as soon as the record button is pressed.

This is especially the case with younger children, but particularly girls, who perhaps have more issues with body image and vanity. There are also issues with child protection and perhaps you need to agree that the video will be immediately deleted after the session or if you plan on keeping the footage for subsequent workshops. This needs to be agreed with the person being filmed and their parents if under 18.

Video observation if used well, can be a powerful tool, as it allows the climber to see what they are actually doing rather than what they think they are doing. As such it fits better with people who already climb to a reasonable level, as the mistakes they are making might well be smaller and harder to gauge in real time. Its use with beginners can overcomplicate what should be simple lessons and mistakes that are probably painfully obvious.

Kinesthetic Observation

The last form of observation can come from the climber you are coaching, through you questioning them to illicit the type of feedback you cannot get from watching and listening. However caution needs to be used with beginners, as if you ask them how a move feels, they have little experience to base a reply on. It is also very easy to lead them to answering what they think you want to hear rather than what is actually happening.

If a student is a long way down the stages of learning then we can increase the questions we ask to illicit feedback. The art of a good questioning is about asking open ended questions, so 'how did that feel?' Might illicit a response of, 'it felt OK'. Having received a reply we now need to follow that up with a more probing question, 'What felt OK or better that time?'

Again the response to that might well lead to a subsequent follow up question. There is a better guide to effective questioning in the Advanced Coaching chapter later.

Analysis

Having observed enough of someones performance we then need to analyze it in detail and try and work out what is wrong. As such there are two sides to the analysis, one is looking for key symptoms of poor performance or common mistakes. The other is then trying to identify the cause of that particular symptom.

EFFECT	CAUSE
Noisy Footwork	Poor foot eye coordination Rushing foot placement
Jerky Movement	Difficulty in putting complex movement together. Poor Balance Anxious Not enough practice
Centre of Gravity out from rock	Poor body or foot position Poor Balance
Face on climbing	Poor body and foot position
Falls off slopers	Poor body position Poor balance
Can't reach handholds	Poor body position Feet too low

Looking at the cause and effect of climbing performance takes experience and deduction. However there are some key things to look out for in climbing performance (see the previoustable).

These are only a small selection of possible effects or symptoms you can see and the possible underlying causes. For a complete rundown of technique coaching, 'How To Climb Harder' by the author and Pesda Press is available in print form only and has many good progressions and tips for a whole manner of climbing movements, alternatively visit snowdonia mountain guides for a CPD course in coaching climbing.

The easiest things to look at when trying to analyze someones climbing technique is the boot, the body and the balance of a climber; The 3 B's. These three parts of the climbers performance can not only effect performance as a whole but altering one will effect the others. Often an effect can be caused by one or more of these 3 B's being slightly off what you are looking for.

Boot - How are the climbers feet using the footholds? Is it effective, can it be made more efficient? Are they using there toe or inside and outside edge? Are the foot placements accurate and precise? Are the feet silent or noisy?

Body - What way is their body facing? Is it appropriate for the move they are trying? Is body position effecting whether or not the climbers hands are straight or bent? Is body position effecting what part of the feet the climber is using? Is the body position effecting how close the centre of gravity is to the wall?

Balance - Is the climber generally in balance? Are

they keeping their centre of gravity close to the wall? Is the movement fluid between point of balance? Does the climber find a point of balance when clipping/placing gear when lead climbing?

For coaches starting out, the analysis of performance can be a daunting thing, as you have to ask yourself am I right and often you cannot answer this until you try and correct someone's technique on your own. In general do not be afraid to try anything, as long as you are prepared to turn round and say that is not working, maybe we should try something else. Again use progression, start out with novices before trying to coach someone to a national standard.

Having analyzed the performance you now need to sort out a way that you can communicate what they are doing wrong and how they can correct it, through the use of feedback.

Feedback

Giving feedback is another hard thing to do, we have to remember that when someone is being coached they can often find themselves in a situation where they hear 'Well that was good, but.....'. After the first few times they will forget what came before the but, and start focusing on the negative aspects of the feedback.

The classic ways round this is to give feedback as a good-bad-good format. Often referred to as the pooh sandwich. "That was really good, but your footwork was a little scrappy, however your body position was excellent". Alternatively it is argued that simply going good-bad is effective as well.

What is important is how you give feedback as a matter of course throughout your coaching by observing constantly. Letting some small issue go by but the moment you see someone doing something well, reward them with a "Great, that is excellent Tommy, your foot work is fantastic". Similarly a simple thumbs up or smile can also have the same reinforcing effect on peoples behaviour.

The reason I say this is as important as giving concurrent positive feedback as a matter of course comes down to a fundamental psychological principal. Positive reinforcement of any behaviour will strengthen that behaviour. In essence the carrot is stronger than the stick, simply saying something positive when someone does something right, will make them more likely to do that exact thing in the future as it will be associated with a reward. We can do this more often than we can go through the whole process of observing, analyzing and feeding back on someones performance.

The next big question is when to give feedback to a student. First of all are you as the coach ready to give that feedback. Have you observed enough, analyzed the performance and worked out in your head how to explain what was wrong and what they can do to refine that performance in a succinct manner? I say succinct, because again we have to think about those 7+/-2 chunks of information the student can process.

Secondly, is the student ready for your feedback?

They might be slowly working things out for themselves through trial and error. They might still be in the earliest stages of learning and trying to get a movement into the ballpark of what you are looking for. They might even be trying to ask themselves questions as to what they are doing and why it doesn't feel right.

There is no sure fire way to tell if someone is ready to be coached on through a skill. Often they may come to you or at the very least look to you for some basic feedback. Those 'Your doing well', "give that another go" can work well. If they do come to you don't miss the opportunity but try to have some structure to you feedback.

Structuring Feedback - Symptom - Cause - Change

When structuring your feedback utilise the symptom - cause change method. Start by describing the symptom of what you saw, with an example of what it is you are trying to correct. Next give a brief description of the probable cause of those symptoms and finally explain what they are going to do to change that.

So to give an example then, you might start by saying "When you did that rockover, your foot banged down really hard onto the hold and missed the best part to stand on. I think this is because you are rushing your foot placements, so you are not being accurate. To improve that I want you to slow everything down and try and make you foot placements silent". The three sentences cover the symptom, the cause and the change.

Other forms of feedback

What we have covered so far in the feedback is that of giving verbal feedback. Again we can also use visual and kinesthetic feedback to help correct mistakes.

Visual feedback, maybe showing the student what they did wrong, by you mirroring their mistakes, then showing them what they need to focus on to improve. Alternatively, if there is someone in the group who's technique is good, you can utilise them as a model for this visual feedback. Similarly can you video the mistake and use the climber themselves as a model to illustrate what they have doing wrong.

A further form of feedback is kinesthetic feedback, in the main this is more aimed at students with the level of understanding of a skill that they understand what feels right or wrong, good or bad. However it can also be used when teaching belaying to complete novices, as by moving the students hands through the 'Take in', 'Lock off', 'Hand Swap' and 'back to the beginning', we can get them into the ball park of that movement through actually feeling what they are trying to achieve.

The final form of feedback was mentioned briefly earlier, in that we can give off many non-verbal signals. Those smiles, facial expressions that we might be unconscious of give a lot away, when it comes to how we are feeling. A look of disappointment or joy, as a climber succeeds or fails will be picked up on by the students, but it can be hard to mask.

Summary of the Session

In this part of the models we are looking to bring our session to a conclusion. There are many ways to go about this, one is to highlight what the students have done, why you got them to do it and where they can apply those specific lessons. Again this is using the same four **W**'s of What, Why, When & Where, that we used in the introduction.

Another alternative is to get the students to review the session by asking questions. Start off by asking them what they did in the session and if you can write down on a whiteboard or a piece of paper what they did. What we are doing is getting the student to use the periodic memory by remembering the order of the day.

Once the students have recalled the order of the day by remembering what they did. The next step is to go into each part in more detail by asking questions about why they did it, as well as when and where they can apply it. This second part uses there semantic memory to associate skills with appropriate places to use it and any caveats or learning points to the skill's use. Again this gets the students involved actively in forming their own conclusion under your guidance.

Finally, thank the students for there efforts and frame their achievements by pointing out how they improved over the session. Where they were at the start and where reached by the end. Again focus on the positives.

Advanced Model

Hopefully by now you realise that whilst the models at the start of this chapter give an excellent framework with which to start from. When new to coaching using them can help you to include all of those points. However as you develop as a coach all that is really important is that at some point during the coaching session you include the following:

- **Introduction**

- **Demonstration**

- **Explanation**

- **Effective Practice**

- **Observation, Analysis and Feedback**

- **Time to correct through more Effective practice**

- **Conclusions**

The order in which they appear and the frequency of the observation, analysis and feedback, followed by the correcting practice can change. In particular looping back through effective practice, observation, analysis and feedback, before having the student try again is a very important part of more advanced coaching. Often the number of loops is only governed by the students learning, if they are making headway then it is working, when they start to plateau its time to move on.

We can use this plateauing to add contextual interference to their learning by getting them to practice one thing for a period of time. When your student's performance stops improving stop that activity and work through another skill. Again when they are showing signs of leveling off in their performance either return to the first skill or add another skill before returning to the original skill. This interference ensures that the learner then extracts the lessons from a previous session from their long-term memory. If you like a much larger scale form of augmented practice. Again it is a great way to run sessions on consolidating skills.

In adding this interference to learning we force the learner to reconstruct or maybe even elaborate on prior learning, helping them develop a much more robust skill.

Teaching/Lesson Plans

Another form of tool to help you develop better coaching and teaching is the use of lesson plans. How they are useful to start with is they involve you sitting down and planning a session before you deliver it. Whilst you might well have observed another coach deliver a session completely spontaneously, like every skill they may well be in the autonomous stages of learning when it comes to coaching climbing.

As such we can apply the learning theory to our own coaching development. As such when starting out it is good to plan and prepare properly for each session, as it will lead to a better product for your students. Before long you will develop generic lesson plans in you head for certain skills that you teach often and be able to amend them to fit different groups and situations. However to start with the more planning you give your sessions the better they will be.

Do not think the lesson plan is just for novices even experts use lessons plans especially when teaching complex skills or courses. Although they may include less detail and may only include a simple list of progressions. This means the coach doesn't have to be thinking about what they are doing next whilst they should arguably be observing their clients performance. Similarly if it is a whole day or week long course, planning it out allows better time management.

In this example I am going to use teaching belaying as the aim of a small session, however this will no doubt take up only one small section of a much longer session.

Lesson Plan for teaching belaying

Title: Teaching Belaying

Objective: To teach students to belay a climber up a route and lower them off safely.

Assumptions: Climbers have already successfully put on harnesses and tied in.

Resources: Two adjacent easy top rope routes, 2 belay plates and two HMS carabiners.

Time: 15 minutes

Introduction: What belaying is

Why we need to do it as instructed.

Can we ask these as questions to get more activity done by the group?

Demonstration: A silent demonstration of the belaying technique.

Followed by asking what I did

Group talk through the component parts, as I perform each step.

Explanation: Add in descriptions of actions. eg.

V- Knee - 1 2 3

PLUS (Pull - Lock - Under - Slide)

Take in lock off hand swap

Activity: Each person has a turn at belaying, with each team staggered so for the first time each person belays they are closely observed and backed up by me the coach.

Look for everyone completing one belay as prescribed (Getting them into the ball park).

Common Mistakes and feedback:

Are they overreaching when taking in.

Are they locking off.

Are they hand swapping correctly.

Feedback via guiding their hands through the process, at first until pattern develops.

Use overt instructional description - Take In, Lock Off, Hand Swap, back to the beginning. (alternatives are V, Knee, 1, 2, 3)

On the second attempt at belaying has each belayer improved from the first. Is there less input from me the coach?

Coach still backs up all students throughout session.

Summary: They have achieved a complex task of belaying each other safely. They need to do much more practice and need to be backed up by their peers as well as possibly the instructor.

Review: We will cover this in the reflective practice chapter, but typical questions are.

What Happened?

What were your thoughts and feelings on the effectiveness of the session?

What was good/bad?

What else could you have done?

What would you change next time?

Summary

In this chapter we started by looking at the basic teaching and coaching models. All of which give us a framework with which to start out coaching. However as the chapter progressed we looked at the essential component parts of those models and by the end suggest that the rigid frameworks are great for starting out. As a coach progresses in their own understanding of the coaching process they may well loop through various aspects of those component parts in any order to achieve better learning outcomes.

Like any skill, coaching using these principles is something that takes time and deliberate practice to master. By using these models of teaching here you can in effect apply it to your own skills to develop as a coach.

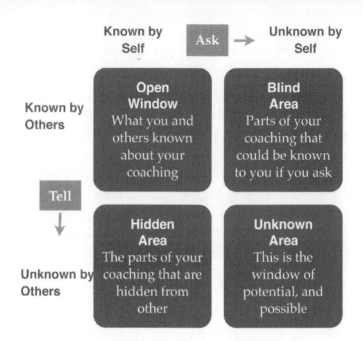

Known by Self → **Ask** → Unknown by Self

Known by Others

Tell ↓

Unknown by Others

Open Window
What you and others known about your coaching

Blind Area
Parts of your coaching that could be known to you if you ask

Hidden Area
The parts of your coaching that are hidden from other

Unknown Area
This is the window of potential, and possible

6 - Advanced Coaching Skills

So far we have looked at what is broadly considered skill acquisition, however a climbing coach may well work with a team or a small group of climbers over a long period. In this section we look at developing a 'team' and how to maintain a good coach-athlete-parent-club relationship and more advanced questioning techniques as well as the legal and moral issues of coaching climbing.

Introduction

Whilst we have covered the basics of the coaching process when aimed at skill acquisition, there are many other aspects of coaching behaviour that can effect our teaching. These are behaviours that are aimed at helping us become more effective communicators, leaders and team builders.

In general these new skills are to do with the development of better coach-athlete relationships, team development and the Long-term development of a climber. Like the skill acquisition elements of coaching process, these are skills in themselves and by applying the learning process to them you can develop these attributes of better coaching. The first element we are going to explore is advance communication, before moving onto Developing teams, Fostering Coach-Athlete relationships, the process of mentoring other coaches, and finally the legal and moral aspects of coaching.

Advanced Communication

Whilst how to ask questions might not seem like that complex a skill to develop, knowing when to ask and what type of questions to use can enhance your coaching.

At their most basic questions can be open or closed. So "Did that rockover feel good to you?", can limit the response to a simple yes or no. As such the question is closed.

Whereas, if you ask, "How was that rockover?", you instantly open up more complex responses, although the response could be another simple answer like, "It was OK", although they might respond "It was good and felt smoother than before". As such the question was more open ended.

That initial question if possible should be open ended and not leading. So avoid making a statement before a question, like "That rockover looked smoother, how did it feel to you?". This will immediately prime the student to respond to your statement, as whether they mean to or not many students will seek to give you answers they think you want to hear.

The real art of questioning comes in the response to those initial questions. So "How was that rockover?", "It was OK", needs to be followed up by a more probing question like "What was OK about it?", "How was is better?", "How could you improve it?". Basically you are taking their answer and rephrasing parts of it as a new question.

Sometimes it can take a long series of their response and you reframing that response as a question to get down to the detail you were trying to elicit from a student. Remembering all the time that we don't want to necessarily lead a student to the answer instead getting them to answer their own questions, will in essence help teach them to self-coach. This often means pausing and thinking between questions.

There is one other form of response that comes from the realm of counselling. It is often referred to as the universal response. Whereby a student might try and attribute a certain aspect of performance to every aspect of their climbing.

An example might be "Every time I climb I get scared?", here the student has subconsciously applied being scared to all their climbing. The key words to look out for are every and all type words that makes a statement general rather than specific.

The classical response is simply to throw that statement they made straight back at them for clarification. "Every time?". The hope is by throwing back a sweeping generalisation they have made gets them to re-examine the statement and in return make it more specific.

So the response might be, "Well not every time, but when I am on routes that are at my limit, I find myself getting scared."

Now we have more detail, so we can ask "Where specifically on the routes, do you find yourself getting scared?"

"Generally towards the top and when I am getting pumped"

"When you are at the top and getting pumped, what is it you get scared of?"

"Well, I not scared of falling off, but I do get scared that I won't be able to hold on long enough to place gear or clip the next bolt or the lower off."

In this little example of the questioning process,

hopefully you have seen that through well thought out and structured questioning we have gone from a generalised, I am bad at everything, to a specific, I am just scared of not being able to clip when I am pumped and near my limit.

As well as the universal response some people posit 'mind-reading' responses, like, "My Coach thinks I am useless". In such they have tried to read their coaches mind. Again a classical response is to challenge this statement with questions asking HOW, "How Specifically?", "How do you know that?"

Another helpful form of questioning are called TED questions where you invite the person to:

- Tell me about...

- Explain that to me...

- Describe it to me..

As well as asking the right questions it is also important to listen as well and show you have listened. So having spent the time listening to a student you can show you have listened and clarify what you think they meant by using responses like.... "if I understand you right"...."What your saying is" or "is that how you mean it?". Other ways to show you have listened are "So you feel"..."It sounds like"... "You're wondering if"... "You're feeling"... "It seems like"... "You're thinking perhaps". The common element in all these listening responses are 'YOU'. We can also show empathy towards a student by starting a statement with "It must be hard...".

The final part of effective communication is that of non-verbal communication and whilst I don't wish to cover this indepth there are two small parts I wish to cover one is body language and the other is a part of NLP which looks at gaze response.

Body language has two continuums, open and closed with a persons limbs or body. Where open is facing you or no limbs crossed, and closed is being side on or with limbs crossed. The second continuum is forwards and back. As such there are four major stances a person can have when they are communicating with them.

Open and Forward - Shows reflectiveness, the person is engaging and accepting and there might be an opportunity to move things forwards.

Open and Back - Reflective, the person is thinking so give them time to process the information.

Closed and Back - Disengaged, the person is wanting to escape, try to acknowledge their feelings and let them set the agenda.

Closed and Forward - Combative, the person is actively resisting what you are saying and there is conflict that needs resolving.

The final part of this is more of an interesting aside, that has limited support scientifically, but it can help build rapport. It is to do with the language that the student uses and trying to mirror it in some way. Sometimes people will use words that reflect hearing, seeing or understanding. "I see where your going...", "I hear what you saying". Similarly they might use words that reflect one of these senses, and as such you should try and use similar language in the reply.

Further to this NLP suggest, but again it is not well supported scientifically that a right handed person will have a gaze reflect to a question. So when you ask a question their eyes will shift away from you as they search for an answer, where the eyes go to gaze momentarily is said to represent different parts of the brain.

Up and Right - Visual Recall - They are recalling a visual memory.

Up and Left - Visual Creation - They are creating a visual memory.

Left - Auditory Creation - They are creating a conversation.

Right - Auditory Recall - They are recalling a conversation.

Down and Left - Kinesthic, checking feelings. - They are trying to remember how something feels.

Down and Right - Having an internal dialogue.

All of these communication tools take time and practice to master. You may have to constantly look back at this section as you master each type of questioning before moving onto the next.

Developing Teams

Whilst for many climbing coaches the development of a team may not seem to important, there are a growing number of local, regional and nation youth and adult climbing teams. Whilst we can develop an individuals skill through the coaching process already discussed in this book, there are benefits of developing a strong team.

The three aspects of teams I am going to focus on here are, leadership which can be totally different for managing a team or a small group of climbers. Team cohesion, how well bounded the team are and finally the collective confidence of a team or group. All of these attributes of teams have been shown, if developed properly to enhance the performance of not only the team, but as a result the individuals that make up that team.

Leadership

There are many aspects to leadership and many classical models out there that many people understand. Perhaps the easiest of the simple models is of a democratic leader versus an autocratic leader, Genghis versus Gandhi. At one end of the spectrum we tell people what to do and at the other we ask them what they like to do, with a whole array of sub steps in between. It is a very simplistic model and one that works well in outdoor leadership situations where at times we need to be very autocratic due to the serious nature of the terrain. Similarly when the terrain is easy we can switch back to being more democratic.

You can add to this model by having a few new attributes, the so called Laizez Faire leader who lets anything go, as they are so laid back.

Another leadership style is the salesman, who makes people think they are making a democratic decision, but actually they are skewing decisions in their preferred direction. "Well we could spend ages training our stamina or we could go have a great time working strength on the boulders". Whilst it is giving options it is very leading.

What these leadership styles represent is a simple refection of different attributes and arguably a good leader will not fit into one box, but spend their time moving from box to box as the situation dictates.

More recently though there has been much more research into the types of leadership behaviour that is linked to success not only as a business leader but also as a sports coach or team manager. One of the better and easier to understand is called Transformational Leadership.

Transformational Leadership

Is a process where leaders and teams work together to achieve greater levels of success, motivation and morality. It has six dimensions and each one can be consider as an attribute that you as a leader can choose to develop.

- Inspirational Motivation

- Appropriate Role Modelling

- Fostering the Acceptance of Group Goals

- Individual Consideration

- Intellectual Stimulation

- Contingent Reward

- High Performance Expectations

If we now look at each of these dimensions, we can further examine how and why they effect good team work.

Inspirational Motivation, are you as the leader doing what you would like your group to do. Being a keen climber might well inspire your team to follow you. Although it does not necessarily mean you have to be achieving great feats of climbing just that you are either training or pursuing a passion similar to what you would like your students to follow.

The same is true of **appropriate role modelling,** if you want your team to turn up on time, with the right kit and in the right frame of mind to train. Then you need to do the same. This might mean you leave 'emotional baggage' in the car when you turn up to training. It might simply mean that you carry on a focused and determined approached from the moment the session starts to the second it ends. Even putting in an extra time here and there to show your commitment will soon rub off on the rest of the team.

Fostering the acceptance of group goals, is slightly tougher, as it requires setting up goals for the team.

This might be as simple as getting the team to write a contract of behaviour that you and they must abide by. More complex goals can also be set, like number of sessions a week, what the training goal is for the month and how each person in the team can help themselves and others reach that goal. Whatever goals are chosen, getting the whole team involved setting them will make the team more likely to accepted them.

So if you were going to spend a month training power endurance on routes, then you might have each person belay another person for 45 minutes of a session and then swap over who's doing the leading. As such members of the team need to accept that to reach that goal they have to belay for 45 minutes at a time.

The next aspect is **individual consideration** as despite being a team that group is made up of individuals. As such we cannot develop the team without bringing everyone along at the same time. One of your team may well be consistently late, but that lateness comes from the fact they have to travel further to get to a training session. As such you might allow them more leeway than someone who only has to travel a short distance.

Similarly, you might have three hot shot climbers in your team and many other climbers. By ensuring you are spending your time equally among the group and focus the training to each individuals rather than just a few will make all the climbers feel part of the team.

Intellectual Stimulation, is both getting the members of the group to consider their current performance and behaviour. In doing so you can then ask them to reflect on how they can adjust it to improve. It is also about providing enough information to the students so they can make those considerations about their performance more easily. As such using the reflective practice model with more advanced students should help make them think more carefully about their performance.

It could also include getting in outside experts in performance physiology or sport psychology to talk to the team about their field. In essence giving your students as much information as possible to help them develop their own ideas.

Contingent reward is another key ingredient and comes down to the fact that any behaviour that is rewarded will become stronger. Essentially the carrot is stronger than the stick, in that punishing bad behaviour will not necessarily be as effective as rewarding the good.

This is particularly interesting if working with groups with challenging behaviours, the chances are they will have heard, "no, don't do that" for the majority of their lives. So in letting minor issue go and instead focusing on praising the smallest bit of good behaviour can help promote the behaviours you are looking for. Although safety is always paramounts. Similarly, don't raise your voice, if the group is not listening, stop and let them talk, they are wasting their own time, not yours, you have been paid to be there whether they climb or not.

Returning to more regular groups the type of reward

may well vary, if someone has put a massive effort into a session and they want to go off and try a boulder problem they have been projecting. Then maybe the reward for trying so hard is for them to be let off for some free climbing on a bouldering wall. What is important is you let them know that decision came down to their effort in training, not an easy way out on your part as a coach.

Similarly, encouragement is a key aspect of this and it should become an underlying feature of your coaching that you praise any effort in training wherever possible. Thanking the group regularly for turning up and trying so hard is an almost effortless thing to do and its effect will be small, but it will improve your relationship with the group or individual.

As such the reward doesn't have to be in the form of a prize like a bar of chocolate for the best improver of the month. Although having a monthly prize for most improved, most helpful, greatest effort or best lob, might well add further motivation to the team to perform to get further recognition. What is important is that you set these monthly awards up so that different people can achieve them each month.

The final dimension is **high performance expectations,** in that if you only expect your team to do so well, then they will only reach that level. By having high standards that are within reasonable levels, you can push the idea that everyone is capable of achieving great things if they apply the required effort.

Again this might simply be expecting the group to turn up to a training session well hydrated and having eaten a couple of hours prior to training. It might be a level of behaviour you expect the group to maintain.

In particular though high performance expectations and inspirational motivation have been shown in at least one study to be linked to higher performance by teams in a sporting setting.

By looking at each of these dimensions individually you as a coach might see that you need to develop and enhance some aspects of your own leadership. In turn this will help the team as a whole. We will cover this later in the reflective practice, although it is worth returning to this transformational leadership section on its own to develop the leadership aspect specifically.

Teamwork - Group Cohesion and Collective Efficacy

First lets define these two facets of team work. The cohesiveness of a team, is best described as its ability to stick together and remain united in achieving the group goals. Whereas Collective Efficacy, is the confidence of the group to carry out the tasks it has set itself.

Higher levels of both have been link to better performance of a team in a variety of different team sports and whilst even in climbing competitions the individual performs in isolation the support of a team will no doubt have impacts on their performance. Remember Team GB in 2012!

As well as this performance or outcome, there are

other measures more akin to personal and social development of individuals that are just as important. By getting people to work better as a team or small group is perhaps more important than climbing performance.

Collective Efficacy

"A groups shared belief in its own collective ability to organise and execute a course of action required to produce given levels of attainment" Bandurra - 1997.

Bandurra, showed that collective efficacy has 6 antecedents, that affect the groups confidence in the tasks they are set, these are in order of importance:

- Prior Performances as a group.

- Vicarious Experience or Witnessing a group work well together.

- Group Size.

- Group Cohesion.

- Group Leadership.

- Verbal Persuasion

Prior performance as a team may come down to getting the group to visit other climbing clubs for 'friendly' competitions. Similarly it may involved developing some form of modified practice. Where you set up a training session to model an actual competition and get those not climbing to shout encouragement to the group. It could just be as simple as getting the group to train together regularly.

Alternatively when going or preparing for a competition you can help the group to recall their previous experiences and point out the really good signs of teamwork and mutual support the group displayed. This is a form of recollecting prior performances.

Vicarious experience is similar to prior performance but is more about witnessing someone or a group perform well and taking away from that experience of seeing a team do well. Things like how they responded to difficult situation, how they respected each other and how the group encouraged and supported each other no matter what occurred.

Group size is often something that we as coaches have no control over, we will often have a set number of people on our team. The larger the number the harder it becomes to balance individual versus team aims and goals.

I am going to skip the **group cohesion** and cover that in another heading in a moment. However if you suspect that the team is low in cohesion, then often to start with you need to work on individual players confidence to perform, as research has shown teams in low in cohesion it is better to develop the individual confidence as it has a much bigger impact on team performance than collective efficacy or team confidence. Whereas if cohesion is high then a much greater percentage of performance comes down to that groups collective efficacy or confidence than that of the individual. The development of self confidence is covered in the mental skills book. As the subject requires a much more in depth look.

We have already covered how we can develop our **group leadership** via the transformational model.

The **verbal persuasion** aspect of the collective efficacy, is about encouragement and combating negative thoughts. How we achieve that is first as a coach we need to be the leader when it comes to praising good behaviour and of course giving encouragement when people are climbing. However getting the team involved supporting each other is another way we can help 'persuade' climbers to perform 'beyond' themselves and maybe reach just one more hold before they fall.

I once got four climbers to climb a circuit until failure on there own, with no one watching or shouting encouragement. 5 minutes later I got them all to do the same thing, but had the other three shout encouragement. On average the encouragement help them stay on the wall for nearly twice the original time.

The strength of a teams confidence is of vital importance when it comes to their performance. It can help overcome anxiety, buffering against its effects.

Group Cohesion

Again group cohesion can be another important part of not only developing collective efficacy but also a team's performance. When it comes to developing the teams cohesiveness you needs to examine what it is we mean by group cohesion. As it is often measured on two major sources of cohesion, Group Integration and Individuals Attraction to the group. Both of these are then assessed by the social aspects and the task aspects of the team.

- Group Integration to the social side of the team - is whether or not the team integrates socially outside of the activity.

- Group Integration to Task - is the team is united in trying to reach its performance goals.

- Individual Attraction to Social aspects of the group - are my best friends are on this team.

- Individual Attraction to Task aspects of the group - I like the style of climbing in this team.

There are all sorts of ways that these aspects can be used to increase performance and often dependent on the level of expertise of the team, the age of the team and the type of sport, different factors of cohesion are better or worse to foster a cohesive team.

One of the more general rules is that women will often find that focusing on the social aspects of a team will foster greater cohesion, whereas men prefer to be more task orientated.

The important thing is that if you identify an area that the team needs to work on to improve their cohesion, then the solution needs to focus on that aspect. So Group integration aspects need to involved the whole group, whereas the Individual attraction to group may involve just a few members of the team. Similarly social problems can be solved through fostering social interactions beyond the realm of the sport, as well as using climbing as a vehicle to promote better social interactions. Finally task aspects need to be solved by using specific tasks or by setting group goals.

Fostering Coaching Relationships

If we are to work long term with a group or individual it is important that we develop a good working relationship. Often this needs to be worked out from the earliest opportunity and starts with laying out what you expect from them and what they can expect from you.

Essentially we want to lay down some ground rules from early on and explain what we as a coach can do with the resources we have and what we cannot. This is vitally important if you are going to work with a client over an extended period, as ensuring that expectations are well matched will prevent problems down the line.

These problems often arise when there is an imbalance between the coach and the athlete and this relationship is classed as the Coach-Athlete Dyad.

Much of this research has looked at how well matched coaches are with students and students with coaches, often covering a meta-perspective. By that we might ask a athlete what do you think of the coach, this is the direct perspective. We can also ask what do you think the coach thinks of you this is the meta-perspective. As such we are trying to get the coach or client to not so much mind read but answer how they perceive they are seen by each other.

It will be impossible for a coach to elicit these responses from a client, however a third party might well help to uncover places where the coach might think the athlete is doing really well, but the athlete actually thinks the coach thinks they are not performing to their best. By getting both the client and the coach to attempt to 'mind read' each other we can find out much more about how the coach or athlete feels they are being perceived by the other. This approach is only really recommended if there is a real issue between a coach and climber. A qualified sport psychologist would be your best port of call if you suspect a problem between a coach and student.

All of this is avoidable through open discussion between the coach and the climber. However in many case there are other parts of the coaching structure that need to be kept in the loop. So if you are coaching for a club or a wall, then there might well be a senior instructor or coach who needs to be kept informed. When teaching children we also have to bear in mind that parents may want to be told about their child's progress.

How we achieve keeping all parties up to date on students progress is very much on the move. There is currently a website the author has developed call iCoach Climbing and it allows registered users to log their climbing and registered coaches to monitor their clients. Where that progress can be graphed, logged and accessed via the internet. Similarly a club newsletter in the form of an email might well be a modern way to help everyone stay on the same page.

One more simple way to understand how we can be blind to aspects of other people when engaged in coaching is through the Johari Square.

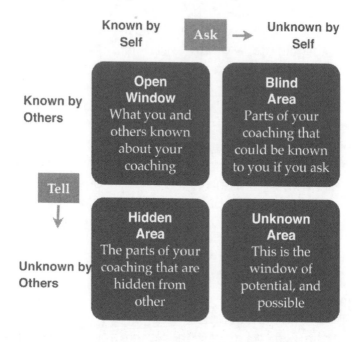

The Johari square suggests we have several windows, into which you or others can view aspects of self.

The Open Window, is what we know about ourselves and others know about us. It can be applied to our coaching, as the diagram suggest, but also it can be applied to developing teams as well the individuals within it.

To increase the Open Window we can get the group member to tell us some information about themselves that others do not know. In essence they are making the Hidden Area smaller by disclosure. However, many people guard themselves from exposing this Hidden Area.

Similarly there are parts of a person that they are blind to, these might be behaviours that a person is unaware of and does not know how that can effect the people around them. Often an individual has to ask others about themselves to find out about these Blind Areas.

In both of these aspects of either asking or telling, it is important that there is trust among the team, so they can appreciate that there is no malice in the answers. When it comes to telling someone what they do has a negative effect on people it might be better coming from you the coach rather than a peer. As it might seem less directly personal. By both asking and telling the open window is enlarged

The other way to enlarge the open window is to explore the Unknown area. This is achieved through either self or shared discovery. As such the Unknown area is often the window of opportunity, as it can lead to revelations about the individual or your own coaching. However this window is the hardest to unlock as it content is unknown by you or your clients.

Mentoring and Supervising other Coaches

In the UK there are a new set of qualifications that are aimed at coaching climbing, this booklet covers the coaching process part of that syllabus and will help see you through all the awards.

However one part of the scheme is that coaches who are going through the scheme will need to be supervised and mentored as part of the qualification process. As such the ability to supervise and guide people will become more and more important. To a certain extent, no matter what qualification a coach has, the more experienced you are as a coach then the more you can offer others from your experience and knowledge.

Again, first of all when taking on a new coach to either supervise or mentor, it is important that you layout what you expect from them and what they can expect from you. If they are working for you, then there will be many requirements in terms of best practice when it comes to maintaining a paper trail either in hard copies or through email and online communication.

A mentor does not have to be a higher level of coach than you, although someone with more experience or a difference set of experiences can bring new or different forms of coaching practice to your attention.

At its most basic a mentor is a person who you can turn to in order to bounce ideas off or a first port of call if something is not working. What the mentor can do is offer advice from a neutral stand point. In that whilst you as a coach could go through the reflective practice process that is highlighted in the next chapter, you are more invested in the experience and perhaps less open to explore various aspects of your coaching practice. If we look back the JoHari square the mentor can help up reduce the size of our blind and unknown areas.

How a mentor can help their coaches, comes down to applying the observation, analysis and feedback models that apply to coaching any skill. Through a process of observing another coach in practice they can then start to analyze and prepare feedback on their performance. For a coach starting out on the coaching journey, their coaching behaviours will be easier to just observe. As they are more likely to be making more obvious errors or overt behaviours that the mentor can help them address.

For a more advanced coach there are probably more subtle areas that can be improved. In order to find these, it may require the mentor filming the coach in action, so a more detailed analysis can be made from observations made on the video. This also allows the mentor to highlight any behaviours with the coach through the playing back specific examples.

Things to look for depend on what the coach is wanting you to analyze. Do they want you to explore their 'coaching process' or observe their communication skills. Similarly they might want advice into how they present training information or exercises to the group.

Like any coaching though it needs to be established what you are wanting from your mentor and what the mentor is expecting from you the coach. What form is the feedback going to be in? Formal or informal? Written, verbal or both?

Also how is the mentor going to help you move on. Will they help you make an action plan? Will they run a CPD session for you and others? How will they follow up the mentoring? Telephone, Skype Facebook,

MSM or email?

What is important is that you appreciate that both mentoring and being mentored is an important part of the coaching process. Neither the mentor nor the coach knows everything. By engaging in the process knowledge is better shared between coaches and coach educators, so we can we strive to become the best coaches we can be. That desire to improve our coaching is covered more in the next section on reflective practice.

Mentoring Opportunities

If you are a aspirant or existing coach, then the author of this book also offers Mentoring opportunities for any coach or instructor via his coaching business snowdonia mountain guides or via iCoachClimbing. com. Mark has numerous experiences both practical and academic. As such he bridges the gap between academic understanding and practical implementation, making him somewhat of a 'Pracademic'. Mark can offer advice and guidance from many divergent areas of coaching and would look forward to learning and developing his own coaching from you as well.

Legal and Moral Aspects of Coaching Climbing

With teaching climbing comes various responsibilities that we the coaches must address. Some of these are moral issues and some are legal issues. At its worst if you cause the serious injury of a climber you are coaching you may find yourself in court defending your actions. What this section is about is trying to develop an ethical coaching practice that is aimed at avoiding injury and harm to your clients. If you like a coaching version of the doctors hippocratic oath.

Whilst much of this is aimed at outdoor climbing, the same can be true of indoor climbing. The reason we have added responsibilities, is that by taking on the role of a coach or instructor we are taking on an enhanced duty of care towards both our clients and those who might be effected by our coaching.

In the UK we owe a duty of care to everyone around us, whether we are a coach or not. This principle was first introduced by a legal case in 1932 between Donoghue vs. Stevenson. During the case Lord Atkin's established what is referred to as the neighbour principle, when he stated:

"There must be, and is, some general conception of relations giving rise to a duty of care, of which the particular cases found in the books are but instances. ... The rule that you are to love your neighbour becomes in law you must not injure your neighbour; and the lawyer's question: Who is my neighbour? receives a restricted reply. You must take reasonable care to avoid acts or omissions which you can reasonably foresee would be likely to injure your neighbour. Who, then, in law, is my neighbour? The answer seems to be - persons who are so closely and directly affected by my act that I ought reasonably to have them in contemplation as being so affected when I am directing my mind to the acts or omissions that are called in question."

The most important part for us then is the definition of neighbour and that we must take reasonable care to avoid acts or omissions which you can reasonably foresee would be likely to injure your neighbour. Today lawyers use a three stage test to assess whether a duty of care is owed.

- The harm which occurred must be a reasonable foreseeable result of the defendant's conduct;

- A sufficient relationship of proximity or neighbour-hood exists between the alleged wrongdoer and the person who has suffered damage;

- It is fair, just and reasonable to impose liability.

That duty of care also changes with the age of the clients we are working with. Under 6s have no responsibilities for their own actions. From this point on there is a sliding scale of responsibility all the way up until someone turns 18. Only at that exact point does all the responsibility come down to the individual and not you, their parents or carers.

As coaches then when we work with anyone below 18 years old we take on the responsibility of In Loco Parentis. Which roughly translates from the legal term as acting or operating as a reasonably prudent parent would act. What a reasonably prudent parent would do in any given situation is debatable, but it is often best to be over cautious rather than under.

As well as age, the level of care we owe someone will change with their experience. A novice will require a higher duty of care than an experienced climber. How you judge that experience is up to you, however it is the experience of the author that some people lie about their experience. In general I have found that men will sometimes give the highest grade they have ever climbed whilst women will often give the average grade they climb at the moment. As such we can never take verbal experience on face value, instead we need observe the level of skill of an individual in a controlled environment. So get the client to demonstrate their skills before you set them off on a more risky lead climb.

So far we have been talking about the duty of care between normal people towards all other people who are covered under the neighbour test. However by being qualified or simply defining yourself as a climbing coach or instructor you take on an enhanced duty of care because you have a declared higher level of experience than the lay person. That duty of care extends to us, our groups, our employer, the organisation groups are from, other outdoor user and arguably the industry as a whole.

I say calling yourself a climbing coach as there is no legal requirement in the UK to be qualified, as under Health and Safety Executive guidelines there are four ways that you can show competence for a specific role.

- Nationally recognised qualifications,

- Equivalent qualifications or accreditation,

- In-house training/accreditation,

- Experience.

Either way if you are calling yourself a climbing coach or instructor then having one or more of these ways to show you are qualified and experienced in the field will help you if the worse happens.

There are several reasons for this, the first being that by being qualified you have undergone suitable training and assessment. In doing so you will have been shown what many might consider as 'normal' practice. In that you do what is considered standard practice within the industry when teaching climbing. As such someone who just has 'experience' as a form of competence may not be aware of what constitutes standard practice.

Using standard practices in coaching climbing will help you avoid the main risk of legal ramifications from an incident or accident that occurs whilst you are working, that of negligence. Although qualifications are not a defense against being negligent.

For someone to sue you or for you to be taken to court on criminal grounds that person needs to show:

- You owed them a duty of care as a coach or instructor,

- That you were negligent,

- That you breach your duty of care.

When being taken to court you will either face a civil court often for damages or a criminal court often in association with manslaughter charges. There is a lesser burden of proof required in civil courts.

There are only two real defences against negligence,

the first is to prove you were not in fact negligent and the second is called Volenti non fit injuria.

Some people may think there is a third defence in the form of a disclaimer signed by the client or the parent. However, the author has worked with a lawyer who was ask to explore the use of disclaimers around the world to see if there was any country a ship could be registered to where a disclaimers against loss, injury or death had been upheld. It is one of the only common threads of global law that no country exists where a disclaimer has been successfully used as a defence against loss of life.

Returning to the proving you were not negligent, by showing that your practices on that day was both 'normal' and 'reasonable'. This will often involve a professional expert witness on both sides. One will argue that your practice was negligent the other will try to defend your actions. If you are only qualified by experience and not by a recognised qualification that covers the activity you were undertaking then this may well be used as a way to highlight possible flaws in your practice. When you are asked what qualifications you have to be teaching someone to lead outside and you say you do not have one, it is not going to look good in court. Other ways to prove you were not negligent are:

- By using proper procedures.

- Checking students ability.

- Choosing appropriate venues and activities.

- Using equipment appropriately.

- Keeping up with good practice.

- Knowing about common accidents and incidents.

- Being appropriately trained and assessed for what you are doing.

Many people instead use the Volenti clause to defend their actions, which roughly translates to a willing volunteer cannot claim for injuries. However to assert that the volunteer willingly and knowingly entered into the activity you have to somehow prove not only that they consented but they were well enough informed about the risks the activity takes to give an informed consent.

A case study from climbing is one of Pope vs Cutherbertson, where Pope was trained over a period of time to know and understand the risks in climbing. Pope fell off lead climbing under Cutherbertson's supervision and injured himself, as a result he tried to sue. The judge found because of the training prior to the incident Pope had enough information to make an informed consent to undertake the activity.

What this means to us as coaches and instructors, especially when teaching leading is we need to ensure that we have covered enough of the basic skills of climbing and the risks it involves to make the clients able to ascertain what risks they are taking when lead climbing.

The author and many other mountaineering instructors have a group talk with people before engaging in lead climbing and highlight the risks. Doing so in front of others means there are witnesses to such conversations. I often say that in tying on to lead climb I see this as them giving consent to the activity. There is a fuller explanation of the soft skills of teaching leading here. However I also need to ensure that I choose an appropriate route and have given them enough skills to cope with that route.

However where the issue becomes very blurred is what to do when teaching children to lead climb. As they lack the ability to legally consent themselves and unless their parents are climbers, do they actually have the ability to give informed consent. You are then left with you as en loco parentis and what decision would a 'reasonably prudent parent' make.

It might be appropriate that if you have a young persons climbing club, to organise an open day so parents can see lead climbing in action. Allowing them to make a more informed decision about it. Outside it then becomes an issue of at what point can you trust an under 18 to make rational choices when it comes to lead climbing? Even if I am right next to someone leading, if they slip unexpectedly the only thing you can do is to have checked all the runners are good and that the belayer can hold a lead fall. Other than that I cannot react quick enough to stop a fall, that said I think the number of times I have had a climber fall off teaching leading is far less than a handful in over 8 years of teaching hundreds of people to lead or push themselves through the grades. Above all the belayer needs to be capable of lead belaying as well.

Having taught many young climbers over the years, it again comes down to building up their skills. So whilst you might start by having them lead a route that is both easy for them and well protected. There are a growing number of young climbers that are climbing F7c or harder on sports climbs. As such an E2 might well be easy for them. The important thing is that the risk is manageable through the quality and quantity of protection available.

There has been at least one incident of a coach taking a young climber out headpointing routes. Whilst at present nothing bad has happened, hopefully you can see through the arguments I have put forward that in doing so the coach is potentially on thin ice. As it is not common practice to introduce lead climbing through headpointing. Arguably some of the routes fit into a category of do not fall off. Given the clients some coaches are working with maybe they are justified in their actions, similarly there are probably headpointable routes out there that fit a description of hard and protectable which may be more appropriate for this approach?

However the legal system certainly does not like harm being caused to young people. As this side of coaching develops maybe we will see a different approach. However at present it is both an ethical and legal grey area.

A final defense is what is referred to as a cessation of cause. Where you might be responsible for someone breaking their leg but it was a complication in the hospital that led to that person losing the use of their leg. As such you were not the direct cause of them losing the use of a leg.

Insurance - A moral Obligation?

If we are going to coach and instruct people in the risky sport of rock climbing then we should be insured. Many of the decisions we make should be based on not only the legal ramifications but also on our own moral integrity. Whilst in the UK there is no legal need to be insured it should be a moral responsibility of every coach or instructor. As if you were found to be responsible for someones serious injury would you not want them to be compensated appropriately for the damages you caused? Similarly if you have a house and no insurance then you could expect to lose it if you are successfully sued for negligence.

If you believe that is the case then you can get various forms of insurance. In terms of protecting you professionally against your potential negligence, then you need professional indemnity insurance, there are however different kinds of insurance:

• Professional Indemnity Insurance

• Vicarious Liability

• Employer Liability

• Self-Employment Insurance

If you work as a sole trader for yourself then professional indemnity insurance will protect you against civil cases for negligence, liable or damages. Usually up to £5 or £10 million pounds.

Vicarious Liability is when you are working for a larger organisation. Often you will be told that you are covered under their insurance. Even if you are the person who is negligent, a claimant often prefers to take an organisation rather than a person to court.

The third type of insurance is for if you run a small business that uses other instructors. As such you become the bigger organisation that is likely to be sued. As such you might want to ensure that all your staff are covered under your own policy. Although many organisations like this also require individual coaches and instructors to be covered by their own insurance. Often if a case is successful the insurer might pursue you as an individual to recuperate some of its payout from your own policy.

Self-employment liability, is generally seen as cover for you should you become ill, injured or otherwise unable to work. As such it is much more optional as it has no bearing on negligence or someone suing you.

Accident Case Studies

As well as Pope vs Cuthbertson there are several other legal cases that have shaped the outdoor industry in the UK over the last 40 years.

1972 - Cairngorm Disaster

A teacher and an instructor headed out to a remote bothy on an isolated plateaux with 12 students. In whiteout condition they failed to find the hut and became lost. Digging into basic snow shelters by the morning seven were dead. It was a spark to develop more relevant qualifications although back in 1972 there was a limited litigation culture. It did result in a greater culture of risk avoidance and qualification uptake.

1995 - Lyme Bay Disaster

A small group of students went kayaking with an unqualified instructor who was poorly trained. The kayaks did not have enough buoyancy, the group did not have spray decks and there was no procedure for groups that were over due. This resulted in a 4 hour delay between when the group should have returned and the rescue being initiated.

In total five students died and it totally changed outdoor education, so now to lead groups of under 18 year olds on various activities the centre or organisation needs an Adventurous Activities License.

The manager of the activity centre was successfully prosecuted for corporate manslaughter. To this day one of the few occasions a criminal case for corporate manslaughter has been used successfully.

1999 - Scout on Snowdon

A volunteer leader was guiding a group of scouts up Snowdon. One of the group became detached from the rest of the group on the way down and the child fell to their death.

The leader was taken to court for involuntary manslaughter and was found innocent, mainly because he was operating as a volunteer. As a result the scouts changed their policy on suitable people to lead groups in the mountains. Which means now as a minimum the leader must have completed their Mountain Leader Training and be assessed by an suitable person in the scouting association.

2009 - Pool Jumping Death

A centre in scotland who had gorge walking on its list of licensed activities, in which some pool jumping activities existed. Over time some of these jumps got bigger and bigger but the centre failed to inform their technical expert that the jumps had changes.

Despite one member of staff raising concerns after a near miss with another member of staff the activity remained. Eventually a twelve year old fell nearly 10 metres onto rocks below and died.

The scottish inquest is extremely condemning of the activity and the fact that alarm bells were raised before the incident brings up the question of whether the incident was indeed foreseeable.

Avoiding Unnecessary Risk

There are many ways to avoid these type of incidents, often having both risk assessments for activities and guidelines for instructors and coaches is of great benefit. Not only to help foresee possible problems but also show a paper trail of due diligence when it comes to risk management.

There was an incident at a climbing wall, where someone injured themselves and part of the judgement came down to the fact that the climbing wall kept poor records of how well trained their instructors were as well as poor equipment logging. In the judgement the poor records where used to highlight a cavalier attitude to risk management. As such keeping well maintain records of both equipment, your on going professional development and experience are vital if you are later required in court to demonstrate that not only were you qualified but your experience was relevant and up to date. Logging experience might be pertinent to someone who has not used their qualification for several years.

Risk assessments are also key to this process and whilst a qualified instructor or coach will have been assessed in there ability to dynamically assess the risk they find. Having a formal risk assessment that is seen and signed off by your staff, as well as regularly reviewed will again help show that you or the business you work for take risk management seriously.

Typically risk assessments look at likely risks, the chances of that risk happening, the likely consequences should that incident occur, how you can reduce the risk and/or consequence and change in likelihood and consequence as a result of mitigating actions.

Likelihood is scored out of 5, 1 being very unlike and 5 almost certain to occur. Similarly consequences are scored on a 1 to 5 scale with 1 being minor (cuts and bruises) and 5 being death. A score of four or above on either is very concerning and should be addressed by some form of mitigation. Which hopefully brings the residual scores down to acceptable levels. A full guide to risk assessment can be found on the HSE website.

Risk	Likeli-hood	Conse-quence	Mitiga-tion	Residual Likeli-hood	Residual Risk

Another way to assess risk is the five lemons model. This comes from New Zealand where a review of outdoor incidents made them realise that is was not just one thing that led to the majority of accidents. Instead it was often a series of bad decisions or lemons that lead to the disaster. Each bad decision is a step closer to reaching five lemons on a fruit machine, if you get five in a row you do not hit the jackpot instead you are perhaps only moments away from the critical mass of disaster.

A final analogy for devising risk management strategies is one that comes from industrial safety. Where a careful assessment of incidents, accidents and near-misses has shown there is a ratio between these. This is often referred to as Heinrich's Ratio. In it they found that for every accident with major injuries there were 29 accidents that caused minor injuries and 300 accidents that had no injuries.

As such some have antidotally seen this as an iceberg, where the 10% of the accidents that have injuries are the part of the iceberg above the sea and that which we can see. The rest of the minor accidents and near-misses are often hidden from view.

If there are only ever a handful of major incidents to learn from, then focusing on these is not the best way to avoid all foreseeable accidents and incidents. If however as coaches we look at the near-misses or minor accidents then we have far more ways to learn from previous mistakes.

As such if you run a small business, it is worth having a near-miss reporting book and encouraging your staff to use it. It can be very daunting for a coach or instructor to use this book. However if you can develop mutual trust and anonymity then these can be very helpful. Other ways around this are to keep an eye in the press or through member organisations like the Association of Mountaineering Instructors or the Mountain Training Association for reported incidents that can also help inform your risk management strategy.

In the future there will be an anonymous incident/accident report form on iCoach Climbing where by any coach, instructor or leader can highlight an incident for the eyes of other instructors totally in confidentiality.

Child Protection Policies

In the UK and many other countries there are now legal responsibilities for organisations and business that deal with children or vulnerable adults to have a formal protection policy for these groups of people. As such if you are working with groups of children or running a kids climbing club then YOU and YOUR business needs to have a Child and Vulnerable Adult Protection Policy.

If the club is voluntary, then in the UK the BMC will often allow you to use their Child Protection Policy. Although it is highly recommended that you develop your own and have some form of training and signing off procedure for all instructors and coaches that come into contact with children. This will help protect the children, the coach and the business. It is also required that a recent eCRB (Enhanced Criminal Records Bureau Check) disclosure form be attained for each coach.

There are many resources online that can be freely taken and addapted to your specific needs. The NSP-CC have a very good policy they encourage people to use and The Child Expliotation and Online Protection Centre (CEOP) is a branch of the police that deals with these issues. Similarly the author developed a child protection policy for his coaching website that was adapted from both of these resources feel free to use it.

Possibly the most important things with a protection policy are that first you have one. Then you ensure that your staff have read and understood it, through either reading the policy or giving staff training on working with youngsters and specific problems like putting a harness on young children, spotting young children and what to do if a child discloses they have been abused and are at risk from someone either outside or inside your organisation.

It is this disclosure that is one of the main emphasis of a policy, in that your policy should name two people who are responsible for child protection, as it means if one of those people is accused then another person can be contacted independently. As well as contacts in the organisation it is also invaluable to have contacts with both local police and local council, both of which should have child protection officers who are trained to deal with these situation.

As such most policies have aspects of what responsibilities a coach or instructor has should abuse be disclosed to them. In a way giving them a road map of who to tell.

All child protection issues are highly emotive and whilst a coach might well have an opinion on the guilt of another, it is important to remember that very few climbing coaches are trained to deal with these issues. External help from the police or local council needs to be gained at the earliest opportunity. It is then up to them to make a case to identify wrong doing and possibly follow up the report with a criminal court case where guilt or innocence are established.

It is of paramount importance for coaches and adults to ensure children are protected from harm.

Summary

Hopefully this chapter has pointed out further refinements to our coaching through greater communications, as well as how we can develop small teams

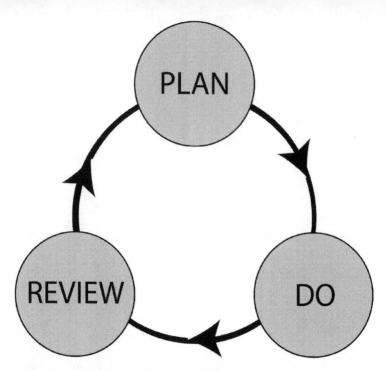

7 - Reflective Practice

Part of being a great coach is reflecting back on your lesson and accepting that not all lessons and classes will run smoothly 100% of the time. By reflecting on the good and the bad points of a session we can improve our coaching game. This chapter looks at a variety of methods to review your coaching practice.

What is Reflective Practice

Reflective practice assumes that you are open enough with yourself to admit that no one is perfect and their is always something we can do to improve our coaching, be it our knowledge or behaviour. It takes a brave step to accept that you are still a work in progress and that there are always things to learn.

It is more than just accepting we can improve but reflective practice is a process whereby we constantly and methodically assess our performance. Questioning what it means and regularly feeding back those lessons into our coaching.

Most coaches and instructors reflect on their work, whether that be subconsciously or deliberately. What reflective practice does is formalise that process and give it a structure and methods to record those thoughts.

If you need more answers to why we should reflect on our practice then consider these points.

- All professionals need the opportunity to grow and develop.

- All professionals want to improve

- All professionals have the ability to learn.

- All professionals have the ability to take control of their own growth and development.

- People need and want information about their

own performance.

Coaching in Action

Whenever we coach, there are numerous things that influence what we do and how we do it. These can be broken down into eight influences on our coaching in action:

- Social Norms - What am I expected to do?

- Values - What do I want the students to take away?

- Prejudices - Why don't I teach the bowline?

- Experiences - This method works 95% of the time.

- Aesthetic Knowledge - How we react to learner and situations?

- Ethical Knowledge - Why I don't use a campus board in coaching?

- Personal Knowledge - I understand who I am and why I react the way I do.

- Empirical Knowledge - What science is there that underpins what I am coaching

Each one of these influences has an effect on our coaching and often as we acquire new knowledge and gain experience our coaching will change to reflect this. Understanding that these do influence us as coaches is a first step to realising the knowledge we have.

Often as coaches we are triggered to reflect on our practice as the result of an event that makes us question some of these influences. Often these triggers are negative, that session went badly but why? That person was closer to their limits than I would like when they are on lead, so why did I chose that route? One of the group let go of the dead rope when belaying, how can I prevent or mitigate against that in future?

If we are triggered by a negative event then we can often find the right question to ask and use our knowledge and experience to answer those questions.

However, we can learn a lot more if we learn to ask different question more often.

What and When to Reflect

We will generally carry out that reflection either during the session or after. There are of course pro's and con's with either method.

Reflecting whilst working as a coach can allow you to immediately change something that is not working. It also limits the amount of time for that reflection as you are engaged in coaching. Reflection after the fact, can give you much more time to explore all facets of what you are questioning and also allows you to seek answers from other sources. For the best results then reflection both when in action and post action need to occur.

The knowledge we gain through reflection can fill one or more of three possible purposes of knowledge; technical, practical and critical.

The Technical knowledge we can explore is about coaching in a more technical role and would include thoughts on personal competency in those roles, the standards you meet to carry out that role and the mechanical aspects of your coaching. An example might be do you have the background knowledge in climbing movement to satisfactorily coach more complex movements or was your goal setting session based on best practice and your understanding from the literature.

If the reflective practice comes from wanting to fulfill a practical knowledge role, then the reflection is more aimed at exploring how you perceived the situation personally. As such it is about what preconceptions and prejudices you might bring to coaching and how they effect you and your clients feelings and actions. If you like it is about asking yourself why you acted like you did in that situation, with that client, on that day. Similarly it might be just exploring the limitations you face from employers, resources and venue.

Finally, the reflection of critical knowledge is about exploring the values and actions. It is about what you might find yourself doing out of habit. As such it can be harder than other forms of reflection as it can involve challenging not only your own habits, but potentially those of larger organisational structures.

Reflective Questions

Some simple questions to get you started are:

What is my coaching like?

Why is my coaching like that?

How has my coaching come to be this way?

What aspects of my coaching practice would I like to improve?

Whose interests are being served or denied by my coaching practice?

What nourishes my coaching and what constrains it?

What pressures prevent or hinder me from coaching in an alternative way?

What alternatives are available to me right now?

The 6 staged model of reflection

Another model for reflective practice is the 6 stage model of reflection developed by Gibbs, 1988. It is aimed at moving you through a cycle that explores knowledge, feelings and behaviours of coaching.

1. Description - What happened during the session.

2. Thoughts and Feelings - What were you thinking and feeling during this session.

3. Evaluation - What was good and not so good about this session.

4. Analysis - What sense can you make of this session.

5. Conclusion - What else could you have done in this session

6. Action - If a similar session arose again, what would you do differently?

John's Structured Reflection Procedure

Johns (1994) develop another reflective practice procedure to implement in nursing. It is also applicable in other fields and is another model to help you reflect formally on your coaching practice. The questions below were adapted from that procedure.

Description of Coaching

Describe the 'here and now' of the session - where it was, when it happened and what happened

What factors contributed to this experience

Who was involved in this session (Clients, employers, parents, etc...)

Having explored the session in detail, what are the key points you need to focus on during this reflection.

Reflection

What was it I was trying to achieve?

Why did I coach as I did?

What thoughts, feelings and previous experience influenced my actions?

How did other people, organisations, time or other external factors influence my actions?

What sources of knowledge did/should have influenced my coaching in the session?

Consequences of Actions

What were the consequences of my coaching and what did I learn about myself, clients and colleagues?

How did I feel about this experience when it was happening?

How do you think the climber felt and how did you know?

Alternative tactics

Could I have managed the coaching session better?

What other choices did I have?

What would be the consequences of these choices?

Learning

How do I feel about this coaching experience?

How have I made sense of this experience in light of past experiences and future practice?

Note down the key lessons from this session in a coaching logbook!!

Reflective Practice in Action

There are numerous ways to implement reflective practice, one of the best ways to start is by reflecting on every session you teach from as early as possible. This way you get into good habits quickly and they should stay with you forever. Just like any skill having a framework to work through like those mentioned already means that eventually reflection will become more automatic and less structured.

How you can go about this is by adding some form of reflection to your logbook of coaching. Mountain Training UK (MTUK) has specific logbooks for all mountain based activities. However they are mainly there to report and describe the days. However that does not mean you can't add in one sentence on reflection or more if the session needs it.

In trying to help develop the idea of reflective practice the author of this book created a coaching website iCoachClimbing.com which has facilities where you can log both your personal climbing, training and instruction/coaching. The logbooks are an online version of the MT UK logbooks. In addition to a form that allows you to fulfill all the needs for the awards, there is also a reflection field and some advice and top tips for each specific logbook area including what questions to reflect on specific to what is being logged. More than this the reflection is also encouraged in your personal climbing as well.

iCoach Climbing has also added a way to log any wider reading, Continuing Professional Development and research you make into any aspect of climbing. By getting you to reflect on what you learnt and where and when you could use that knowledge.

By using these regularly and having easy access to them via any internet connected device, it is hoped you will try to use them every evening after you have been working to help promote reflective practice in action. As well as keep a dynamic and up to date logbook of your work that may well help in furthering your career. These logbooks are free to use for any coach.

Asking Questions

Whilst we can often find answers by asking ourselves those questions of reflection. Sometimes having an independent point of view will be even better. Whilst I covered the idea of mentoring in the previous chapter, it is also an important part of reflection.

This is because the person you are asking the question is emotionally removed from the situation. By removing an emotional connection to the coaching you can often get much better feedback and advice.

Whilst having a head instructor or coach to ask is great not everyone has access to this kind of help. You may have friends or colleagues who you think are more experienced than you or other coaches who have a greater knowledge base in a specific field you need help with.

Often being brave enough to ask someone is the first big step. As it can feel like you are admitting a lack of knowledge or other skills. However, the chances are even those really experienced coaches have had similar experiences in the past and they too were once starting out and needed a nudge in the right direction.

I can remember working as a trainee and had found a problem one day when teaching on a multipitch route. I came back to the staff room and asked a more experience instructor about the specific problem. He said yes that it can be common and I have found that if I do X it can help. Another instructor overheard and said I had a similar problem the other week and I did this. Before I knew it I had four different opinions on the same problem and could learn from their experience.

All were totally unbiased and had slightly different ways to solve the same problem. Unless I had admitted the problem first to myself and then to these more experienced coaches, I might have taken a few more sessions to understand and manage the problem.

On UKBouldering.com they have a closed forum for coaches you have to ask to join. There are also numerous blogs run by coaches and I am sure that if you emailed them with a real question then you will get a reply. If you emailed me at climbing coach I would probably make an anonymous post out of my reply to share the knowledge. If you are a member of the Mountain Training Association (MTA), they too have forums for instructors and coaches

Conclusion

Whilst we have covered many of the more complex aspects of reflective practice and to a certain extent you would not be expected to go through a complete John's Structured Reflection Procedure after every single session. It may well be of use after a particularly difficult session.

Similarly, having a coaching mentor can help to reflect on certain sessions, as to a certain extent they are emotionally detached from the session and can often offer unbiased, uncluttered feedback.

However, don't think that the best coaches simply do the same thing, over and over. Having worked in the national mountain centre and other large outdoor education centres, I can assure you that these 'expert' coaches, analyze and discuss there session on a daily basis. Indeed they are probably assessing it as they are delivering it and certainly when the group are sat down eating lunch those coaches are deciding how to amend the afternoons plan based on the reflecting on what went on in the morning.

They may be gliding gracefully like a swam across a lake through their day. Under the water their brains are paddling like mad to give their clients the best day they can and provide the best learning opportunities for the individuals involved.

This chapter is based on "Reflective Practice for Sport Psychologist: Concepts, Models, Practical Implications and Thought on Disseminations" A. Anderson, Z. Knowles, D. Gilbourne - The Sport Psychologist 2004

Index

Printed in Great Britain
by Amazon